PENGUIN BOOKS

The 24-Hour Wine Expert

JANCIS ROBINSON has been called 'the most respected wine critic and journalist in the world' by *Decanter* magazine. In 1984 she was the first person outside the wine trade to qualify as a Master of Wine. The *Financial Times* wine writer, she is the author/editor of dozens of wine books, including *Wine Grapes* (Allen Lane), *The Oxford Companion to Wine* (OUP) and *The World Atlas of Wine* (Mitchell Beazley). Her award-winning website, www.JancisRobinson.com has subscribers in 100 countries. In 2017 *The 24-Hour Wine Expert* won a Gourmand Award.

KT-149-950

The 24-Hour Wine Expert

Jancis Robinson

Inspired by *Wine Expert in a Weekend*
by Hubrecht Duijker

PENGUIN BOOKS

For Rose,
who shaped, encouraged and guided this book

PENGUIN BOOKS

UK | USA | Canada | Ireland | Australia
India | New Zealand | South Africa

Penguin Books is part of the Penguin Random House group of companies
whose addresses can be found at global.penguinrandomhouse.com.

Penguin
Random House
UK

First published 2017
014

Copyright © Jancis Robinson, 2017

The moral right of the author has been asserted

Set in Swift Neue LT Pro 9.5/13pt by Penguin Books
Printed in Great Britain by Clays Ltd, Elcograf S.p.A.

A CIP catalogue record for this book is available from the British Library

ISBN: 978–0–141–98181–9

www.greenpenguin.co.uk

MIX
Paper from
responsible sources
FSC® C018179

Penguin Random House is committed to a
sustainable future for our business, our readers
and our planet. This book is made from Forest
Stewardship Council® certified paper.

Contents

Welcome

I've been writing about wine for forty years, but every day I learn something new. So I'm not surprised to find that many people find the subject of wine a bit daunting. The aim of this book is to share my knowledge with you and make you a self-confident wine expert in 24 hours by stripping away the non-essentials and concentrating on what really matters.

The best way to absorb all the information in this book is with friends, perhaps over a weekend or on several evenings, and with as many different wines as you can assemble. The more comparisons you can make, the more you will learn. Throughout the book I suggest useful tasting exercises your group may like to undertake, with everyone bringing one or two bottles of the wines proposed. Make sure you have some food to hand – not only for the sake of enjoyment, and for learning which combinations of food and wine work, but also to temper the effects of the alcohol. You won't become an expert if you can't remember anything …

A standard bottle contains 75 cl of wine – six generous glasses, eight perfectly respectable ones and up to twenty tasting samples – so you could form quite a large tasting group. For any unfinished bottles, I give tips on how best to store wine leftovers on pp. 51–2.

If you don't want to organize a wine tasting, use this book to answer your questions about wine as they arise. I suggest, for instance, what sort of wine glasses are likely to give you the most pleasure, how to choose a bottle from a shelf or wine list, whether and how to match wine and food, how to decode a wine label, and how to learn the essentials of wine as quickly and easily as possible.

This book was inspired by someone else's brilliant idea. Hubrecht Duijker is the best-known Dutch wine writer, and one of the more popular of his 117 books is called *Wine Expert in a Weekend*, in Dutch.

All these words and the structure of the book are mine rather than Hubrecht's. But both of us are hugely conscious of the fact that, because wine is now one of the most popular drinks in the world, many, many wine drinkers want to know more about it–without devoting the time and money needed to understand every minute detail and becoming wine professionals. I hope that by sharing my knowledge I can help you get the most out of every glass and bottle.

Jancis Robinson

Some Simple Explanations

What is wine?

> **My take**: wine is the most delicious, stimulating, varied and infuriatingly complicated drink in the world. It cheers you up, makes your friends seem friendlier, and tastes great with food.
>
> **The official EU definition**: wine is the alcoholic beverage obtained from the fermentation of the juice of freshly gathered grapes, the fermentation taking place in the district of origin according to local tradition and practice.

How is wine made?

Fermentation is the key. Under the action of yeast, many sugars can be fermented into alcohol and carbon dioxide. Apple juice can be transformed into cider. Malted cereals can become beer. Even leftover jam can start to ferment.

Grape juice becomes alcoholic when the sugar in ripe grapes is transformed into alcohol and carbon dioxide in the presence of yeast, either the so-called ambient, wild or indigenous yeasts that are present in the atmosphere, or more predictable specially cultured and selected commercial yeasts.

As grapes ripen they gain sugar and lose acidity (and become less hard and less green). The riper the grapes, the more sugars are available to ferment into alcohol and the stronger the resulting wine, unless fermentation is stopped early and some sugar is deliberately left in the wine to make it taste sweeter.

Hotter climates tend to produce grapes with lower

acidity and more sugar, which, if the fermentation is completed, will produce wines that are stronger than those from cooler regions. So, the hotter the summer, the riper the grapes and, usually, the stronger the wine. This is why wines made far from the equator tend to be lighter in alcohol. Wines from Puglia on the heel of Italy, for example, are much more potent than those produced in the far north of Italy, while the fledgling (but fast-improving) English wine industry makes wines notably high in acidity.

Once fermentation has transformed sweet grape juice into the alcoholic liquid we call wine, it may be aged before bottling – especially if it is a complex, age-worthy red. Fruity, aromatic whites are often bottled only a few months after fermentation to preserve the fruit and aroma, but more serious wines may well be aged for a further year or two before bottling to marry their different components, most often in containers of various sizes and ages made of oak, a wood that has a particular affinity with wine. The newer and smaller the cask, the more oak flavour will be absorbed by the wine. The fashion today is to minimize obvious oakiness, so older, larger oak containers, or even neutral ones made of concrete, are increasingly common. Easy-to-clean stainless steel tanks are most commonly used for wines designed to be drunk young.

Red, white or rosé?
Red The flesh of virtually all grapes is greenish-grey; it is the skin of the grape that determines the colour of the wine. Grapes with yellow or green skins cannot make red wine. Wine is red only if dark-skinned grapes are used to make the juice that becomes wine (known as the 'must'). The thicker the grape skins and the longer the juice or must is kept in contact with them, the deeper the colour of the red wine that results.

Rosé Most rosé is made pink by leaving the juice in contact with dark grape skins for only a few hours. Rosé is sometimes made from a mix of pale- and dark-skinned grapes, and occasionally from a blend of already fermented white wine with some red. This is an increasingly respectable wine category, and rosé is now drunk throughout the year rather than only in summer.

White Pale-skinned grapes can only make white wine, although with very careful handling, avoiding contact with the skins, it's possible to make a white wine from dark-skinned grapes. This is sometimes called a Blanc de Noirs, notably in Champagne. Some white wines are made orange by being left in contact with the skins.

What's in a name?

Traditionally, wine was called after its place of origin, its so-called 'appellation': Chablis, Burgundy, Bordeaux, and so on. But from the mid twentieth century, when new wine regions outside Europe were establishing themselves, more and more wines came to be labelled not geographically but varietally, with the name of the main grape variety from which they were made. Thus labels came to be dominated by names such as Chardonnay, the main grape of Chablis and all other white burgundies, and Cabernet Sauvignon and Merlot, the main grapes of red bordeaux. (NB I use lower case 'burgundy' and 'bordeaux' for generic references to the wines themselves rather than to specific regions/appellations.) See pp. 67–76 for my guide to the most important grape varieties and pp. 78–105 for my guide to the most important wine regions, in which I spell out which grapes grow where.

Choosing the Right Bottle

How to choose wine from a retailer

Surveying the vast range of wine bottles available from most retailers, whether on a shelf or online, can be disconcerting. I give ten tips in the table overleaf, but it's virtually impossible to guide someone to a specific bottle without knowing each individual's personal preferences and without being there with them. In all that I write, I see my key role as giving wine drinkers enough of the right sort of information for them to make educated choices.

When people ask me how to choose wine I always suggest that they forge a relationship with a local independent wine retailer. There are strong parallels between wine shops and bookshops. Just as you can tell booksellers your likes and dislikes so that they can make tailored recommendations, so it is a sound policy to tell an individual wine professional what you like and ask them to recommend something similar but more adventurous, better value or better-made. The supermarkets may have massive purchasing power, but this is useful only for the cheapest of wines, and they all too rarely choose wines on the basis of their quality nowadays. This is why it makes sense to encourage the smaller independents, who really understand and care about every bottle they sell.

To get you going, see the table on pp. 14–15 for slightly more adventurous suggestions, based on 'if you like X, you'll love Y'.

But if you would rather make all your selections yourself, or are perhaps located far from any bricks-and-mortar outlet, then do check out all the sources of helpful information that are now available both in print and online. To find out more see 'How to choose from a restaurant wine list' (pp. 16–17).

Be adventurous

The obvious choice
The clever alternative
(sometimes cheaper, often more interesting)

Prosecco
Crémant du Jura, Crémant de Limoux

•

Champagne
English sparkling wine

•

Big-name champagne
(NM in little letters on the label)
Grower's champagne
(RM in little letters on the label)

•

Pinot Grigio
Austrian Grüner Veltliner

•

New Zealand Sauvignon Blanc
Chilean Sauvignon Blanc

•

Puligny-Montrachet
Chablis Premier Cru

Mâcon Blanc, Pouilly-Fuissé
Jura white

•

White burgundy
Galician Godello

•

Meursault
Fino or Manzanilla sherry

•

Beaujolais
**New-wave reds from Maule and Itata
in southern Chile**

•

Argentine Malbec
Côtes-du-Rhône red

•

Rioja
**Spanish Garnacha, Calatayud,
Campo de Borja**

•

Châteauneuf-du-Pape
**Single-estate wines from
Languedoc-Roussillon**

•

Smart red bordeaux
Douro red

How to choose from a restaurant wine list

There is generally less choice in a restaurant or bar than from a retailer, and the mark-ups are very much steeper (generally from 100 to 300 % on cost price), so mistakes are much more expensive. Historically, the great majority of establishments have relied on making most of their profits from selling alcoholic drinks, the thinking being that people are much more likely to know how much a steak costs than how much a specific bottle of wine costs. However, the advent of smartphones, the website Winesearcher.com, which lists global retail prices, and useful apps such as Raisinable, which scans restaurant wine lists (so far only in London and New York) to identify the lowest mark-ups, means it is increasingly difficult for restaurateurs to pull the wool over consumers' eyes.

If you want to be in control of your own choice from a list, I strongly recommend you take advantage of the many sources of information available to you today. Many restaurants publish their wine lists online, so you can do your research in advance, checking out how each wine that might appeal is rated by well-known critics (ahem) and/or by community websites such as CellarTracker.com.

If you are unable to undertake any research before your visit, you can always take your smartphone with you and quickly look up some of the wines that appeal to you and your guests. (Check out my suggestions for food and wine pairing on pp. 34–7.)

But if you can't make up your mind, or feel under-informed, do the most obvious thing of all: ask the wine waiter, or sommelier, for advice. Contrary to common belief, this is far from a sign of weakness. In fact, I'd go so far as to say that asking advice can be a sign of confidence and expertise, whereas diners who lack knowledge are more likely to be too timid to engage a wine waiter in conversation. Any good wine waiter loves to discuss wine. It was the old brigade, knowing and caring very little about wine, who hid behind a mask of haughtiness. But today's somms, as they often style themselves, are much more likely to be true enthusiasts, ready to make recommend-ations at different price levels. A suitable question, after ordering your food, would be 'I'm looking to spend about X; we generally like Y'; or, 'I'm looking for a red and a white. What would you recommend?' You will make the wine waiter's day.

Don't be ashamed of ordering some of the cheaper wines on the list; only oligarchs and oil magnates who positively relish spending over the odds head for the most expensive end of the list.

Ten ways to pick the right bottle

1. Avoid bottles that have been stored close to strong light (you don't want one from the shop window) or heat sources. This can rob a wine of its fruit and freshness.

2. Look specifically for wines bottled as close as possible to where the grapes were grown. All wine labels have to state the address, or at least the post code, of the bottler, if it was not the same person as the producer. Be wary of, say, a New Zealand wine that was bottled in the UK. An increasing proportion of wine is shipped around the world in bulk, which may be ecologically sensible for inexpensive wine, but really serious wine producers will insist on bottling their wines themselves. Look for 'Mis en bouteille au domaine/château' on French wine labels.

3. If the wine is stoppered with a natural cork, choose one that has been stored horizontally, which keeps the cork damp and oxygen out.

4. Check the fill level in the neck. You don't want a space of more than two or three centimetres above the surface of the wine in an upright bottle, as this would be a sign of too much harmful oxygen in contact with the wine.

5. For fine wines it can be extremely difficult to remember exactly which year is best in which region. A useful shortcut may be my Rule of Five: all vintages since 1985 divisible by five (ending in 5 or 0) have been pretty good.

6. Be wary of back labels that are too specific in their flavour descriptors and recommended food matches. It could suggest an excess of marketing gloss. Personally, I prefer details of how the wine was made.

7. Take your smartphone so you can check the ratings and opinions of critics and other wine enthusiasts.

8. Head for independent wine retailers and ask for advice. If they give you bad advice, try another one until you are happy.

9. For inexpensive white and especially pink wines, choose the youngest vintage available.

10. If a bottle is on special offer, ask why. Sometimes it is because the wine is in bad condition or is too old.

Bottles and Labels

Clues from the bottle

The classic Bordeaux bottle shape is generally used for reds made mainly from Cabernet and/or Merlot grapes, wherever they are grown, and for white wines from Bordeaux.

classic bordeaux bottle

classic burgundy bottle

The classic Burgundy and Rhône bottle shape is very common, especially for reds based on Pinot Noir, Syrah and Grenache grapes and for Chardonnays, but also for a wide range of other wines.

Sparkling wine bottles have to be made of thicker glass than most to withstand the pressure inside them and generally resemble big burgundy bottles, though many of the most expensive champagnes come in their own special shapes.

Bottle sizes

The standard bottle contains 75 cl of wine, which is why wine by the glass tends to come in neat fractions of that volume. Half bottles contain 37.5 cl but are quite difficult to find, as producers a) want to sell as much wine as possible, b) are worried that there is proportionately too much oxygen in the bottle for long-term ageing, and c) know that it costs just as much to fill, stopper and label a half bottle as a full bottle. The wine-trade theory is that the perfect size for stately maturation is the magnum (150 cl), because the ratio between the volume of wine and of oxygen is supposedly optimal. (The counter argument is that a magnum with a duff cork is particularly disastrous.) Even bigger bottles of fine wines tend to be for show-offs.

Clues from the label

I firmly believe that a wine label can take you more directly to an individual producer than is possible with any other product. As the retired adman John Dunkley said when he set up the Tuscan estate Riecine, 'Wine production is the one activity where one person can be in charge of everything from soil to label to sales.'

Domaine Drouhin

DUNDEE HILLS ②

Pinot Noir ③

OREGON

DROUHIN FAMILY ESTATE

① producer ② geographical appellation ③ grape variety

Vieille ① Vigne ②

Gevrey-Chambertin

1er. Cru Clos St Jacques ③

APPELLATION GEVREY-CHAMBERTIN 1er CRU CONTRÔLÉE
④
Mis en bouteille par ⑥
SCEA DOMAINE FOURRIER ALC 13.5% BY VOL
⑤ ⑦
750 ml PROPRIÉTAIRE A GEVREY-CHAMBERTIN (CÔTE D'OR) FRANCE

① means 'old' (an unregulated term) ② means 'vineyard' ③ vineyard where the grapes were grown ④ geographical appellation ⑤ producer ⑥ most wines have to say who bottled them and where ⑦ alcoholic strength

European wine labels, such as Fourrier's Gevrey-Chambertin (p. 21) typically focus on geographical names rather than grape names, relying either on back labels (not often enough) or assumed knowledge (dangerous) to inform consumers about what they are likely to actually find in the bottle.

The Domaine Drouhin front label tells you where the grapes were grown, and what variety those grapes were, but all the detail and mandatory information is on the back label – a common practice, particularly outside Europe.

See pp. 67–76 for a quick guide to the most common grape varieties and pp. 78–105 for a rapid tour of the world's major wine regions.

How strong is my wine?

All wine labels have to state the percentage of alcohol by volume (although American wine labels generally seem to use the smallest font possible for this useful information). I strongly encourage you to take note of this, as it can have a significant impact on how you feel the morning after. A 15 % wine is more than a seventh stronger than a 13 % one. It is worth noting, though, that variations of 0.5 % between stated and actual alcohol content are not uncommon. Producers used to exaggerate alcohol levels when turbo-charged wines were fashionable, but nowadays they are more likely to round the stated alcohol levels down.

As outlined in 'How is wine made?' (pp. 10–11), the hotter a region's climate, the stronger the wines it can produce – although sometimes winemakers, particularly in the relatively cool wine regions of Germany, leave a little unfermented grape sugar in the wine instead of fermenting it all into alcohol, so their sweeter wines may be only between 7 and 9 % alcohol. Most still wines on sale today, however, are between 13 and 14.5 % alcohol, although in warm wine regions, such as Châteauneuf-du-Pape in the southern Rhône, where the local grape (Grenache) needs to reach considerable ripeness before expressing itself fully, wines can easily reach 15.5 or even 16 %.

In most parts of the world, the current fashion is for trying to lower the alcohol content of wine without reducing its flavour and character, so we are seeing an increasing number of wines at between 11 and 13 % alcohol. Because high acidity is a key characteristic of good-quality sparkling wines, grapes for champagne and other sparkling wines tend to be picked a little earlier than for still wines, and the resulting wines are often around 12 % alcohol, while fresh, lightly fizzy Moscato is virtually halfway between grape juice and wine, at 5 to 7 % alcohol.

Generally speaking, the further away from the equator, the lower the alcohol. But in cooler parts of Europe producers are allowed to add sugar to fermenting grape juice to create an additional 1 or 2 % alcohol. This is called 'chaptalization' after Jean-Antoine Chaptal, one of Napoleon's ministers, who dreamt up the process in the early nineteenth century, when it usefully disposed of a sugar-beet surplus.

In a way, this is the opposite of acidification, a technique widely used in warm wine regions (and increasingly permitted in cooler ones after a particularly hot summer) whereby additional acid, usually tartaric (think of cream of tartar), which is found naturally in grapes, is added to fermenting grape juice. Chaptalization and acidification of the same tank is everywhere forbidden.

Average alcoholic strengths

5–7%
Moscato, Asti

7–9%
Mosel wines with some sweetness

9–12%
Drier German wines, deliberately
early picked wines

12–13%
Champagne and other sparkling
wines, an increasing proportion
of still wines

13–15%
The great majority of still wine
on sale today

15–20%
Fortified wines such as sherry, port
and madeira, and stronger Muscats
etc. (see 'Other kinds of wine' (p. 53 – 5))

How to Taste

This is how the professionals taste, and it's surprisingly easy to do in everyday life as well, without being too pretentious about it.

Step 1 – Look at the wine

Tilt the glass away from you, ideally against a white or pale background. Check the colour in the middle of the wine, and the colour at the rim. In maturing red wines, there is often a noticeable difference between the two.

The deeper the red in the middle of the glass, the thicker the grape skins (a sign of a thick-skinned grape variety or a hot, dry summer). A pale orange rim is a sign of a mature red. A young red is typically blueish purple through to the rim, indicating extreme youth.

Both reds and whites go tawnier with age: white wines deepen in colour, while red wines become paler. Ageing a wine in an oak cask, or in contact with oak chips or staves, can deepen the colour of a white wine. Colours vary with grape varieties. See more on pp. 67–76.

Suggested exercise: This won't be cheap, I'm afraid. Try to find two different vintages of the same red wine – preferably more than two years apart – and see how much less purple the older wine looks. Bordeaux should offer the greatest choice.

Step 2 – Smell the wine

This is the single most important aspect of wine tasting. All the **flavour** is perceived as an aroma because our most sensitive tasting equipment is at the top of the nose. (Even if you have never consciously 'nosed', as they say, a wine, you may have sensed some of its flavour because some smell-laden vapour also travels up to the top of the nose from the back of the mouth.) The more complex the flavour, the better the wine.

Trying to attach words to the flavours will help you remember them. In 'Common tasting terms' (pp. 28–33) I include some of the words frequently associated with particular grape varieties, but there are no rules about which flavours you are 'allowed' to use to describe wines. Indeed newcomers to wine often come up with much more apposite and useful flavour descriptors than old hands, because they approach without preconceptions. It's a difficult business attaching words to something so nuanced and subject to individual sensitivities and preferences.

Suggested exercise: Put a diving clip or even a clothes peg on your nose and try to taste a wine. Notice how much more difficult it is if you can't smell freely. You could even get a friend to blindfold you and see whether, with a clip on your nose, you are able to tell grated apple from grated carrot, even grated onion. I bet you won't be able to. This is why food tastes of nothing when you have a blocked nose.

Step 3 – Get a mouthful
The tastebuds inside your mouth give you an idea of the **dimensions** of a wine:

acidity lemons and vinegar are particularly tart, or high in acid; it really leaves a tingle on the sides of my tongue, though I'm sure we are all different in our responses
   acid tasting terms (*from low to high*): *flabby, well-balanced, fresh, crisp, taut, austere, tart, sour, acetic*
sweetness the amount of sugar in a wine can vary from an unnoticeable 1 gram per litre (g/l) to an off-dry 10 g/l to well over 100 g/l in a really sticky one

sweet tasting terms (*from low to high*): *bone dry, dry, medium dry, rich, medium sweet, sweet, unctuous, tooth-rotting, cloying, sickly sweet*

tannin a natural preservative extracted mainly from grape skins found in young red wine (and also in cold tea) that dries out the inside of your cheeks

tannic tasting terms (*from low to high*): *Soft, round, firm, astringent, tannic, tough, hard*

alcohol leaves a hot sensation at the back of the mouth

alcoholic tasting terms (*from low to high*): *light, well-balanced, medium-bodied, full-bodied, big, hot*

In a good mature wine, all these elements are in harmony, meaning none stick out.

Suggested exercises: Taste lemon juice and cold tea (no milk!) to grasp what acidity and tannin feel like respectively. Really take notice of how they affect the inside of your mouth.

Step 4 – Afterwards

The so-called 'finish' or 'length' of a wine is a great indicator of quality. In a good wine the flavour lingers on agreeably after you have swallowed it. Producers of relatively industrial wines put a lot of effort into giving them a striking, if often rather simple, smell but that tends to be it. The taste fades away fast, encouraging you to have another sip just to check there is nothing more. A mouthful of a great wine tends to last much, much longer. An excuse to spend a bit more?

Tasting exercise: Compare the finish of the mature red bordeaux suggested in the exercise for Step 1 with that of the cheapest red bordeaux you can find. The former will last so much longer after you swallow (or spit) it.

Common tasting terms

The following is a guide to terms often used by professionals to describe the dimensions and structure of a wine.

As for specific flavours, there are no absolute rules. We almost certainly all perceive things in different ways, quite apart from having different preferences. Various flavour terms have come to be attached to specific grapes or wines out of habit – such as 'peppery' for Syrah, 'grassy' for some Sauvignon Blanc and 'spicy' for Gewürztraminer – but these are probably professional shorthand. What we are really saying is 'This smells like Syrah/Sauvignon Blanc/Gewürztraminer.'

I give some of the most common flavour descriptors for the principal grape varieties in 'Remember that grape' (pp. 67–76), but, as I mentioned earlier, newcomers are much better at attaching flavour descriptors to wine aromas than tired old professionals who used up their wine vocabulary years ago and can be very sloppy in the way they apply them. You should feel quite at liberty to free-associate. Note which flavours individual wines remind you of, be as precise as possible in identifying similarities with other aromas, and build up a bank of your own helpful descriptors. They will be much more useful than recycling the wine vocabulary of a third party.

acetic so sour that the acid dominates the wine, meaning it is dangerously on its way to becoming *vinegar*

aftertaste what you sense once you have swallowed the wine (or, at a professional tasting, expectorated it); compare *finish*, which is how long the aftertaste lasts

aroma what you smell; flavour and aroma are in practical terms indistinguishable because you can only sense flavour as a vapour via the nose

aromatic particularly smelly – in a good way

astringent lightly tannic: puckers up the inside of the mouth a bit, but not aggressively. Used especially for whites

baked smells as though the grapes got rather hot on the vine

balance perhaps the single most important aspect of a wine. A wine is in balance, or well balanced, if all the dimensions of a wine – acidity, sweetness, tannin and alcohol – are harmonious

body roughly the same as alcoholic strength; potent wines are full-bodied, whereas relatively weak ones are light-bodied, or just light

botrytis technical term for the 'noble rot' fungus that concentrates ripe grapes and produces great sweet wine; smells somewhere between honey and cabbage

bouquet sometimes used for the complex mix of aromas that develops in a mature wine

brett short for *Bettanomyces*, a yeast that can imbue reds with aromas akin to horse or sweaty saddle, or something more like heady cloves

broad seems to fill the mouth nicely

chewy a little bit more tannic than astringent

clean without any perceptible faults

closed not especially smelly but with sufficient concentration and tannin on the palate that it seems as though it will develop more aroma

complex offers several different, well-integrated flavours; bottle age is generally required to deliver complexity

corked/corky smells unappetisingly mouldy, usually associated with a cork tainted by TCA (see p. 38)

crisp has an attractive but not excessive amount of acidity

dried out has lost its youthful fruit to an unappetising extent

extract the density of a wine; a high-extract wine is very unlike water and has a high concentration of solids such as sugars, acids, minerals and proteins. Extract is different from *body*. Many a Mosel Riesling is low in alcohol but high in extract.

finish the duration of the aftertaste; a wine is said to have a long finish, or be long, if it lingers on the palate, but is short if there is no, or hardly any, aftertaste

firm having notable but not

painful tannins

flabby uncomfortably low in acidity

flat without much aroma or freshness

flavour see *aroma*

forward unexpectedly mature and developed for its age

fresh very like *crisp*, but with very slightly less acidity and a definite suggestion of youthful fruit

fruity generally full of fruit(s) of any sort – by no means necessarily *grapey*

full-bodied see *body*

grapey a small minority of wines actually smell like grape juice, most of them made from Muscat grapes

grassy smells of fresh green grass, typical of Sauvignon Blanc

green smells underripe

hard too low in fruitiness

herbaceous smells of green leaves, often found in less than fully ripe Cabernet Sauvignon, Sauvignon Blanc and Sémillon

hollow without enough fruit on the mid palate, i.e. in the middle of the tasting process (see *palate*)

hot delivers a warm or even burning aftertaste, generally the result of an excess of alcohol

inky a personal descriptor for wines that don't have that much fruit but have a bit too much tannin and acidity

legs another word for *tears* (cue jokes about long legs)

length see *finish*

lifted quite but not excessively *volatile*

light not necessarily a criticism; see *body*

long see *finish*

maderized an old wine that is oxidized may be described thus

mature a wine that has clearly evolved in bottle to become *complex* but has not yet started to become *dried out*

mercaptan stinky notes that can be reminiscent of bad eggs but which aeration can help considerably

mid palate see *palate*

mineral much-used, much-discussed umbrella term for flavours that are not in the fruit, vegetable or animal spectrum but seem instead to be more reminiscent of stones, metals or chemically derived aromas

mousey this may indicate a fault

mouthfeel originally an American term for a wine's texture, but now it usually denotes power together with a lack of aggressive tannins

noble rot see *botrytis*

nose the most important bit of our tasting equipment, but tasters also refer to the smell of a wine as its nose, or describe aromas detected 'on the nose'

oaky a wine that has been in contact with oak (whether casks, chips or staves) during ageing is known as 'oaked', while a wine that tastes overtly of oak is called 'oaky'

old pejorative term for a wine that is past *mature*

oxidized wine that has been exposed to too much oxygen, or air in general, and thereby loses its fruit and freshness and is on the way to *vinegar*. This is why care should be taken with leftovers to minimize the space above the wine in the bottle

palate one of the most frequently misspelt words in wine and an umbrella term for an individual's tasting equipment (as in 'she has a seriously good palate') but also more specifically for what happens in the mouth (as opposed to the nose). Wine can make an impact on the front palate at the beginning of the tasting experience in the mouth, on the mid palate, and finally on the back palate. You might also refer to a wine's impression 'on the palate'

peppery black pepper is commonly associated with not-too-ripe Syrah grapes, white pepper occasionally with Grüner Veltliner grapes, and green pepper with underripe Cabernet Sauvignon

petillant lightly sparkling

racy a word I use a lot for wines that seem to have good acidity and real energy and attack on the palate

residual sugar the technical term for the amount of unfermented sugar left in the wine. It is usually expressed as grams per litre (g/l). Anything under 2 g/l is imperceptible; anything over 10 g/l is usually quite obvious, although the more acidity a wine has, the less obvious its residual sugar

rich a complimentary term for

a wine that seems intense and flattering without necessarily being particularly sweet

round without particularly obvious tannin but not dangerously soft

short see *finish*

spicy this term is often misused to describe the distinctive lychee-like smell of Gewürztraminer grapes, simply because in German *Gewürz* means 'spiced'. Some wines do smell of various spices, but it's an umbrella term that is often as imprecise as *mineral*

spritzig very slightly fizzy; some winemakers deliberately leave a little of the carbon dioxide given off during fermentation dissolved in the finished wine. A few very tiny bubbles are not necessarily a fault in white wines, but in full-bodied reds they may indicate that the wine has started to re-ferment – not a good thing

steely usually denotes a white wine with perceptible but not intrusive tannin and acid

sulphur the most common antioxidant used for millennia in the production of wine (and juices and dried fruits). Small amounts occur naturally in winemaking and are harmless to most people, but asthmatics may well react to sulphur, which is why most wines carry the warning 'Contains sulphites'. Heavy concentrations can cause a tickle in the back of anyone's throat. Wine producers continue to use less and less sulphur, although many sweet wines may need more sulphur than most to stop the residual sugar fermenting

supple positive tasting term for a wine whose acid and tannin levels are agreeable and harmonious

sweet self-evident (see pp. 26–7)

tannic pejorative term for a wine that has a bit too much tannin (see 'How to taste', pp. 25–7, for where it fits in in the spectrum of tasting terms related to this wine preservative)

tart a little too acid

tears the streams of liquid you sometimes see running down the inside of a wine glass, especially in higher-alcohol wines. Contrary to popular opinion they have nothing to do with viscosity nor glycerol but are generated because wine is a liquid made up of many different components with different surface tensions. The presence of tears (or *legs*) is not terribly significant

thin lacking fruit and weight

vanilla commonly associated with the smell of American oak

vegetal all sorts of vegetable-related aromas can be found in wine, but this specific term is usually used interchangeably with *green*

vinegar what you don't want to find in your glass of wine; exposed to air and a high enough temperature, wine gradually becomes *volatile*, then *oxidized*, and then out and out vinegar

viscous sticky, generally most common in strong, sweet wines

volatile all wines are volatile in that they give off vapours but as a tasting term this is pejorative and indicates an excess of acetic acid, a major component in *vinegar*

weight just as in humans, a measure of *body*

woody smells of poor quality or badly stored wood, usually oak

'Supertasters'

We all have different densities of tastebuds on our tongues. In the 1990s Professor Linda Bartoshuk of Yale University devised something called the PROP (6-n-propylthiouracil, a thyroid medication) test involving a compound which tastes horribly bitter, mildly bitter or of nothing at all. This test divides the population into 'supertasters', 'normal tasters' and 'non-tasters', according to how many taste buds we have. About a quarter of the population falls into each of the extremes and about half are normal tasters. The terms were subsequently revised to be less judgemental: supertasters became 'hypertasters' and non-tasters became 'hypotasters'.

Hypertasters have a particularly high density of taste buds and are more sensitive to strong flavours and textures. Hypotasters have a low density of taste buds and need extra stimulation before sensing anything. Caucasian women are apparently more than twice as likely as their male counterparts to be hypertasters.

Matching Wine and Food

Far too much fuss is made about trying to find the perfect pairing of wine and food. Choosing any wine is complicated enough without worrying about whether it will go with what you are eating. And anyway, when eating out, and sometimes in, there is usually a range of different dishes on the table.

Much more important than the colour of a wine is its weight in the mouth and the impact it makes on your palate. If you're eating something reasonably delicate – burrata, fresh mozzarella, goat's cheese, an omelette, poached white fish or chicken – it makes sense to drink a fairly delicate, light wine with it: a Vermentino, Chablis, Sauvignon Blanc or a rosé or light red such as Pinot Noir, Cinsault or Beaujolais.

If, on the other hand, you're eating pork belly, hamburger, steak tartare or venison, you probably want a wine that's a bit meaty – a full-blooded wine that really makes an impact on you, such as a rich Grenache/Garnacha, Syrah/Shiraz or Mourvèdre/Mataro.

Matching food to specific wines

There are one or two tricks you can play when thinking about food to match a particular wine:

- If you want to drink a young red that is high in tannin, so still quite chewy, you can make it taste less uncomfortably chewy by serving food that's literally chewy, such as roast red meat or a steak.
- Aromatic, full whites such as Riesling and Gewürztraminer, even pretty fruity ones, can be lovely with spicy foods, especially those with a Thai accent.
- If you want to continue to drink wine with something sweet, do make sure that the wine is even sweeter than the food – otherwise the wine will taste horribly tart and

thin. Real tooth-rotters such as Pedro Ximenez (PX), rich Sauternes, Rutherglen Muscat from Australia or ripe ruby port can fit the bill here.
– Be wary of artichokes; they play tricks on your palate and make wine taste metallic, so avoid expensive wines with them.

Matching wines to specific foods

However sceptical I am about 'perfect pairings', I know people appreciate short cuts, so here are some suggested tried-and-tested combinations. Note how much easier in general white wines are to match with food than reds:

First courses

asparagus tricky, but try dry German or Alsace whites

ceviche tangy Sauvignon Blanc

charcuterie cru Beaujolais, Chianti Classico, good quality Valpolicella, dry Lambrusco–any red with a bit of a bite

chicken liver parfait whites with a touch of sweetness such as Alsace white, Pinot Gris, Condrieu, Vouvray

consommé the traditional accompaniment is a dry sherry or madeira, jolly nice too

crab full-bodied whites from Burgundy, Bordeaux or the Rhône

globe artichokes even trickier than asparagus, because they make wines taste metallic, so nothing special

oysters champagne, Chablis, Muscadet

salads a wide variety of whites should work, preferably one with quite a bit of acidity

shellfish (see also crab, above) whites from the Rhône and the south of France, opulent Chardonnays

smoked salmon Riesling, Gewurztraminer, Pinot Gris

soups these don't strictly need any liquid accompaniment, but you could try whatever would go well with the un-liquidized version of them

sushi and sashimi sake (Japanese rice wine) is pretty good, also champagne

terrines light reds such as fruity Cabernet Franc and Merlot, Chinon and Bourgueil, Pinot Noir

Main courses

aïoli dry Provençal rosé; it really does work

barbecued meats smoky reds such as full-blooded Barossa Shiraz and South African Pinotage

burger something simple, red and fruity – young varietal Merlot?

chicken very versatile, but only the heartiest chicken dishes can withstand really full-bodied reds, and light reds or full-bodied whites are often a better match

daube, casseroles of all sorts southern Rhône reds, mature red Rioja

egg dishes, such as frittata, omelette and quiche runny yolks can coat the mouth and hide subtle wine flavours, but cooked eggs as in these dishes should be fine with soft, light reds as young Merlot and Pinot Noir

fish, pink, such as salmon or tuna New World Pinot Noir can be a great match

fish, white simply grilled or poached white fish is one of the few foods that is pure and simple enough not to overwhelm a light German Riesling, but richly sauced fish dishes can be beautiful with fuller, off-dry whites such as Loire Chenin Blanc

game red burgundy and top-quality Alsace white are the classic matches

pasta Italy's more appetizing reds such as Chianti, Valpolicella and a host of other wines made from Italian grapes

pizza wine of any colour would be a friend to any tomato, but I'd suggest nothing too complex

risotto depends on what's in it apart from rice, but full-bodied dry whites should work

steaks and chops the chewiness of these meats usefully tames the tannins in young reds designed for a long life such as young red bordeaux, ambitious young Italian reds, and Iberian reds such as Douro or Ribera del Duero

truffles Piemontese wines made from Dolcetto, Barbera or Nebbiolo

veal serious Tuscan reds

Cheeses

blue cheeses sweet, full bodied whites such as Sauternes is the classic and highly successful choice

hard cheeses, such as cheddar this can be the ideal foil for a really grand mature red bordeaux or other top quality Cabernet Sauvignon, as well as for mature vintage port

washed-rind cheeses, such as brie tangy, fruity whites such as Jurançon, Vouvray, honeyed Chenin Blanc

Sweet things

chocolate tends to annihilate most wines but very sweet, strong ones such as port, Pedro Ximénez (PX), malmsey madeira and sweet sherry work well

fruit-based desserts sweet Loire whites based on Chenin Blanc such as Vouvray work well, as do most French wines with the word 'moelleux' (meaning '(bone) marrow-like', i.e. of medium sweetness) on the label and many fresh Italian sweet whites such as Recioto di Soave and Picolit

ice cream the chill factor tends to anaesthetize the palate, so nothing too serious; Moscato works well

patisserie any sweet white that is sweeter than the food (any less sweet wine will taste uncomfortably tart)

Restaurant rituals

One of the last remaining rituals of restaurant service is the pouring of a small sample from a bottle of wine ordered for the host of any party to try. I bet the great majority of those who do the trying (and indeed of those who do the pouring) aren't too sure of the point of it, which is for the person who has ordered the wine to check the temperature and whether it has a fatal flaw. I quite often find in restaurants that reds are served too warm (so I ask for an ice bucket) and whites can be too cold (so I ensure the bottle is left out of an ice bucket).

As for the flaws fatal enough to allow you to send a bottle back, the principal one is that the wine smells too mouldy to enjoy. The most common reason for this smell, often called TCA by professionals (short for trichloroanisole, the chemical compound responsible), is a tainted cork. Such wines are often called 'corked' or 'corky'. The problem is that the level of TCA contamination can vary enormously and, complicating an already complicated business, our sensitivities to TCA vary considerably. This can result in some rather heated discussions between waiters and customers, but you could point out that, unless the wine is very old, the restaurant may well be able to return the bottle to the supplier and get a refund. One common side-effect of TCA is a lack of fruit on the palate. Note, however, the important fact that you do not have the right to refuse to buy an opened bottle simply because you don't like the taste.

Two of the most infuriating habits of some waiters are to fill up your glass more frequently than you want, and/or to such a level that there is no room above the wine for the all-important aroma to collect. You will be doing all wine drinkers a service if, politely but firmly, you make your feelings about these practices clear.

Matching Wine to the Occasion

What I love about wine is its variety. Not just in terms of colour, strength, sweetness and fizziness. Not just because of all the varied grapes it's made from and places it's grown, resulting in all those fabulous different flavours. What I like most is the fact that there are wines for every day, wines for smarter occasions, and wines that are designed to celebrate the really special moments in life. I know people who drink nothing but first growth bordeaux and Grand Cru burgundy, but I'd hate to be one of them; I'd really miss my honest peasant farmer wines.

It's much cleverer to match the wine to the occasion than to always serve wine as grand as you can afford. For a barbecue, for example, it would be a waste to serve anything too special. A robust spicy red such as a Mendoza Malbec, a southern Rhône, a Spanish Garnacha or Australian Shiraz would be just the job. For a simple supper, I'd choose an honest but simple wine–a Beaujolais, Muscadet or young Chianti perhaps–from an artisanal producer. But if I'm entertaining really serious wine lovers, I make sure that I serve something that will be a real treat for them.

Crowd pleasers

These are wines that are not extreme in any way, and have shown themselves over time to be capable of pleasing a wide array of palates.

friendly whites

- Mâcon Blanc
- Pinot Blanc (called Weissburgunder in German)
- Chablis
- Albariño from north-west Spain (called Alvarinho in northern Portugal)

- Alto Adige and Friuli whites
- Vermentino
- Falanghina from near Naples
- Verdicchio from Italy's Adriatic coast
- New Zealand Sauvignon Blanc and Chardonnay

friendly pink
- Dry Provençal rosé

friendly reds
- New Zealand Pinot Noir
- Pinot Noir from Australia's Mornington Peninsula
- Côtes du Rhône
- Spanish Garnacha
- Douro reds
- Chianti Classico
- Carignano del Sulcis from Sardinia
- Fleurie, St-Amour, Moulin-à-Vent – top-quality Beaujolais with the most attractive names

Bottles to knock socks off
These are names that would mean something to insiders:
- Bollinger, Cristal, Dom Pérignon, Krug (champagne)
- Chassagne-Montrachet, Meursault, Puligny-Montrachet, St Aubin (white burgundy)
- Trimbach Riesling Clos St Hune (dry white Alsace)
- Equipo Navazos (sherry)
- Niepoort (port)
- Barbeito (madeira)
- Châteaux Grand Puy Lacoste, Léoville Barton, Pichon Lalande, Pichon Baron, Vieux Château Certan (red bordeaux)
- Domaines Dujac, JF Mugnier, Roumier, Rousseau (red burgundy)

- Château Rayas, Clos des Papes, Château Beaucastel (Châteauneuf-du-Pape)
- Massolino Vigna Rionda Riserva (Barolo)
- Vallana (Boca)
- Castell'in Villa, Poggio delle Rose Riserva (Chianti Classico)
- Gianni Brunelli, Le Chiuse di Sotto (Brunello)
- Passopisciaro Contrada (Sicilia)
- Allende, CVNE, López de Heredia (Rioja)
- Arnot Roberts, Au Bon Climat, Corison, DuMol, Frog's Leap, Littorai, Rhys, Ridge, Spottswoode (California)
- Brick House, Cristom, Eyrie (Oregon)
- Leonetti, Quilceda Creek, Andrew Will, Woodward Canyon (Washington State)
- Cullen, Curly Flat, Giaconda, Grosset, Henschke, Moss Wood, S. C. Pannell, Penfolds Grange, Tolpuddle, Vasse Felix (Australia)
- Ata Rangi, Kumeu River (New Zealand)

Bottles as gifts

Don't head automatically for the most expensive wine in a store unless you know the recipient has a wine cellar. They are usually young fine wines that need many years' ageing.

Even wine professionals love to be given good-quality champagne – either one of the luxury bottlings, such as Krug or Dom Pérignon, or a bottle from one of the top growers (see the sock-knocking list above).

Any really obscure but interesting wine, such as one made from a rare grape variety or by a promising new producer (preferably one recommended by a professional), can be a great gift for the wine-lover.

Top-quality balsamic vinegar or estate-bottled olive oil is another common gift between wine professionals.

My favourite champagne growers

These are relatively small-scale producers who grow all their own grapes, with the village in which they are based.

- Raphäel et Vincent Bérèche, Ludes
- Chartogne-Taillet, Merfy
- Ulysse Collin, Congy
- J. Dumangin, Chigny-lès-Roses
- Egly-Ouriet, Ambonnay
- Fleury, Courteron
- Pierre Gimonnet, Cuis
- Laherte Frères, Chavot-Courcourt
- Larmandier-Bernier, Vertus
- Marguet Père et Fils, Ambonnay
- Pierre Moncuit, Le Mesnil-sur-Oger
- Pierre Peters, Le Mesnil-sur-Oger
- Jérôme Prévost, Gueux
- Eric Rodez, Ambonnay
- Suenen, Cramant
- Vilmart, Rilly-la-Montagne

Twenty heart-stopping (and bank-breaking) wines

I see to my amazement that the number of wines on my website that I have given a perfect score of 20/20 to is over 100. Below are the crème de la crème, in the order I'd choose to drink them at one, heart-stopping, fantasy feast.

- Equipo Navazos, No. 15 Marcharnudo Alto, La Bota de Fino NV Sherry
- Bollinger, RD 1959 champagne
- Trimbach, Clos Ste Hune Riesling 1990 Alsace
- Egon Müller, Scharzhofberger No. 10 Riesling Auslese 1949 Saar
- Domaine de la Romanée-Conti, Grand Cru 1978 Montrachet

- Domaine Leroy, Grand Cru 2012 Chambertin
- Domaine Armand Rousseau, Clos St Jacques Premier Cru 1999 Gevrey-Chambertin
- San Guido, Sassicaia 1985 Bolgheri
- Petrus 1971 Pomerol
- Château Cheval Blanc 1947 St-Émilion
- Château Palmer 1961 Margaux
- Château Latour 1961 Pauillac
- Château Haut-Brion 1959 Graves
- Château Mouton Rothschild 1945 Pauillac
- Paul Jaboulet Aîné, La Chapelle 1961 Hermitage
- Penfolds, Grange 1953 South Australia
- Marqués de Riscal 1990 Rioja
- Château d'Yquem 1990 Sauternes
- Quinta do Noval, Nacional 1963 Port
- Taylor's 1945 Port

What your choices say about you

Prosecco: fun, extrovert, unfussy

Champagne: sybarite

Albariño, Rueda, Vermentino, Savagnin: adventurous white-wine lover

Fair Trade wines: compassionate

Wine in heavy bottles: marketing victim

English/Canadian wines: English/Canadian patriot

Red bordeaux: conservative, traditionalist

Hefty Australian Shiraz: bet he does the barbecuing

Natural wine, sherry: hipster

Burgundy: masochist (failure rate can be disappointingly high)

Wine sold for a premium in an ampoule or similar: mug

How Much Should I Pay?

Contrary to common belief, there is no direct correlation between price and quality in wine. Many wines are over-priced because of inflated market demand, ambition, greed or just because a marketing person sees the need for an 'icon wine' in the range. The difference in quality between wines at the top and bottom ends of the price scale is narrower than it has ever been, while the difference in price has never been greater. Clever wine buyers head for reliable examples of underpriced wines.

Packaging, shipping, marketing and, in many countries, local taxes and duties tend to account for by far the majority of the price of very cheap wines, with the cost of the liquid itself representing a tiny fraction of how much you are paying. But ambition is responsible for much of the selling price of more expensive wines. For this reason, the best value is generally in the range of £7–£20 or $10–$30 a bottle. Here, you more or less get what you pay for.

Some under-priced wines

I give below (in italics) a handful out of hundreds of possible examples, favouring those with good distribution. For more, see JancisRobinson.com

- Bordeaux's so-called petits châteaux, those without a famous name
  Châteaux Belle-Vue, Reynon
- Languedoc-Roussillon wines from specific addresses
  Domaine de Cébène, Domaine Jones
- South African whites
  A. A. Badenhorst, Chamonix

- Chilean reds and, increasingly, whites
  Clos des Fous, De Martino
- Loire in general and Muscadet in particular
  Bonnet-Huteau, Domaine de l'Ecu
- Beaujolais
  Julien Sunier, Château Thivin
- Côtes du Rhône
  D&D Alary, Clos du Caillou
- Spanish Garnacha
  Capçanes, Dani Landi
- Portuguese wines
  Quinta do Crasto, Esporão

Some overpriced wines
- Bordeaux's most lauded reds, the so-called 'first growths'
- Burgundy's Grands Crus from the most famous vineyards there (red and white)
- California's 'cult Cabernets'
- Much champagne
- Most wines described as 'icons'

Wines I would pay over the odds for
- Bottles of fine wine that have been matured for years in trustworthy conditions (at a relatively low, steady temperature; provenance is everything for wines like this)
- Great rarities (which excludes the Bordeaux first growths of which hundreds of thousands of bottles are made each year)
- Bottles sold in aid of well-run charities

Ten common wine myths

1. **The more expensive the bottle,
the better the wine**
Best-value bottles retail between £8 and £20.
Below £8 there's usually too little left after fixed
costs and taxes to pay for the wine, so poor
quality is likely. Above £20 and you risk paying
for ego, 'positioning' and the vagaries of the
fine-wine market.

2. **The heavier the bottle, the better the wine**
Wine producers, particularly in Spanish-speaking
countries for some reason, have used thick glass
as a marketing tool, but it is very wasteful of the
world's resources and most top wine producers
are more sensible.

3. **Old World wines will always be better
than New World wines**
There is good and bad everywhere.

4. **You must drink red wine with meat
and white wine with fish**
See 'Matching wine with food', pp. 34–7

5. **Really good wines come in a bottle with an indentation ('punt') in the base**
Punts are often there for marketing reasons.

6. **Red wine is stronger than white**
Many reds made today are only 12 % or less.

7. **All wine improves with age**
See 'Which wines need time', pp. 62–3.

8. **You're given a taste of the wine you've ordered in a restaurant to see whether you like it or not**
See 'Restaurant rituals', p. 38.

9. **Pink wine and sweet wines are for women**
Pur-lease.

10. **All wine is improved by 'breathing' between opening and pouring**
See 'When to open the bottle – and whether to decant', pp. 60–61.

Essential Hardware

Glasses

Wine glasses need not be complicated. They just need to slope inward towards the rim so that you can safely swirl the wine, maximizing its surface area and therefore encouraging all those flavour messages to escape and gather in the space between the wine's surface and the rim of the glass. To provide lots of room for this aroma, it's not stingy, just practical good sense, to serve glasses no more than a half, and preferably only a third, full; a glass with a total capacity if full to the brim of 250–350 ml is ideal, allowing plenty of space for aromas of the swirled wine to linger above the usual serving of about 120 ml.

What helps the swirling – which needn't be so aggressive that it's laughable – is a stem. A stem also allows you to hold the glass without affecting the all-important temperature of the wine (see pp. 58–9). Stemless glasses are all very well for a picnic, and tumblers are supposed to signal that you are in a casual bar or restaurant, but I favour a stem myself.

Contrary to what glass manufacturers may suggest, you don't need more than one size or shape of wine glass. There is no logic to the idea that a white wine should be served in a smaller glass than a red. And professionals are rapidly coming round to the view that even champagne, port and sherry are best appreciated in exactly the same size and shape of glass as unfortified wines.

Standard Riedel

Zalto Universal

48

Champagne was once served in flat coupes, and these have enjoyed a renaissance recently, but the taller the glass, the longer the wine will remain fizzy, because there is a smaller surface area for the bubbles to escape through.

champagne coupe   champagne flute

Wine glasses should ideally be colourless–even the stems–and as plain as possible. Heavy, cut glass gets in the way.

The one thing that can affect the tasting experience is the thickness of the glass. The finer the rim and the thinner and less adorned the glass, the more intimately involved with the wine you feel. Professionals shy away from coloured, engraved and faceted glass for this reason. My favourite glasses are the most basic made by Riedel, the leading wine-glass manufacturers, for everyday use, and, for special occasions and therefore special wines, the super-fine Universal model made by Zalto. Both, thank goodness, are absolutely fine in an ordinary dishwasher.

The packaging — *bottle, pouch, can or carton?*

Wine has been packaged in glass for centuries because it is a neutral, durable material. But bottles are heavy and fragile. Making, transporting and even recycling them also uses up considerable resources. For wine that's drunk within a few months of being packaged there are strong arguments (and I know this may go against the grain) in favour of cartons, pouches, cans or even plastic bottles–all of which are so much lighter. Most of the materials used for these will react with the wine after a few months, so glass is definitely best for wines worth ageing.

Another admirably sustainable development is the increasing popularity of wine shipped in and sold from containers much larger than a bottle such as bag-in-boxes and kegs. The technology has improved enormously so that wine can now be kept really fresh for weeks rather than days. Obviously this sort of packaging isn't suitable for fine wine that deserves prolonged ageing, but it makes perfect sense for the great majority of wine drunk today.

Cork, synthetic or screwcap?

Bottles need stoppers, and for centuries cylinders of cork bark seemed to do the trick – being neutral, durable and perhaps letting in a tiny amount of air to help the wine age. But towards the end of the last century the (mainly Portuguese) cork manufacturers got careless, quality declined, and wine producers started to notice an increase in bottles affected by cork taint, whereby the wine smells unappetisingly mouldy (see p. 38). Worst of all is low-level cork taint that is obvious only to producers, who can see that their precious wine has been robbed of its fruitiness but which is not so obvious to ordinary drinkers that they know they have the right to complain.

The result of all this was that an increasing number of

producers, especially in Australia and New Zealand, where they felt they were sent especially poor-quality corks, started using alternative stoppers such as synthetic copies of corks and screwcaps (which can be designed to allow varying tiny amounts of air into the wine). Cork manufacturers then upped their game, but apparently too late to recapture the antipodean market. It is too early to know how well wine will age under screwcap over centuries, but there have been experiments with wines aged for a decade or two under screwcap, and these are often preferred by tasters to the same wines stoppered with natural cork.

Extracting the cork

Cork devotees decry the lack of romance associated with screwcaps, and worry about the ecosystem in cork forests, but it has always struck me as bizarre that most wine is sold in a container that can only be opened with a special bit of equipment used for nothing else. I refer of course to the corkscrew.

I probably have skewed judgement since I so often have to open dozens of bottles at a time, and therefore the screwcap seems a boon to me. I love the Screwpull and its counterparts, which extract corks with two simple lever movements – but they can easily cost more than £60. The most important attributes of a corkscrew are that the helix is hollow (so that the corkscrew doesn't drill a hole right through the cork, robbing you of any traction) and its point is nice and sharp. See illustrations overleaf.

Opening a bottle of fizz

The pressure in a bottle of champagne can be as much as that in a car tyre, so it is vital to keep control of the cork while opening the bottle. Take the wire muzzle off carefully, holding the cork in the bottle neck with your thumb.

Then twist the bottle slowly off the cork, continuing to hold the cork down until it comes out gently. The cooler and less shaken the wine, the less likely it is to have an unruly and potentially dangerous escapee cork. The racing-driver technique is not advised.

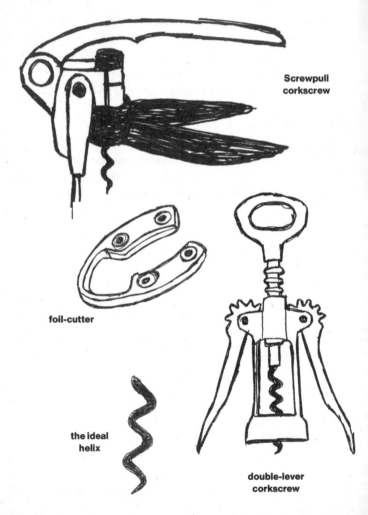

Screwpull corkscrew

foil-cutter

the ideal helix

double-lever corkscrew

Other Kinds of Wine

Sparkling

As grapes ferment into wine, they give off carbon dioxide (see pp. 10 – 11), the harmless gas found in all fizzy drinks – including **sparkling wine**.

Bubbles can get into wine by **carbonation**: the carbon dioxide is simply pumped in (which is what cola manufacturers do).

A more sophisticated, long-lasting method is the **tank method** (*méthode Charmat* or *cuve close* in French), whereby sugar and yeast are added to a tank of wine to provoke a second fermentation. The carbon dioxide given off can be trapped in the wine, which is bottled under pressure. This is how Prosecco from north-east Italy, and most less-expensive fizzy wine, is made.

Spain's Cava and the wines of the Champagne region in north-east France are made by a much more painstaking technique known as the **traditional method**. Here, the second fermentation is provoked not in a tank but in each bottle, so that the wine gains complexity by being in contact with the dead yeast cells, for many months and sometimes years. The resulting sediment is frozen in the neck of upturned bottles and expelled under pressure. The bottles are then topped up and the final cork and wire muzzle to keep it in place are applied. Champagne and its many imitators around the world are based on Chardonnay and very delicately pressed dark-skinned Pinot grapes.

Fortified

Another subgroup of wines are stronger than average and are called **fortified wines**, because they have had alcohol (neutral grape brandy) added. **Port** comes from the Douro valley in northern Portugal and owes much of its alcoholic strength (which is 18–20 %) to the spirit that is added to fermenting local grape varieties long before all the sugar has turned into alcohol. Most port is deepest purple when young, thanks to the Douro's unusually hot summers. The other most famous fortified wine is **sherry**, made from pale-skinned Palomino grapes on the plains around Jerez in southern Spain. A range of different styles is made by varying exactly when and how the spirit is added and how long the wine is aged in the all-important barrels that create each sherry's character. The styles I find most useful (and completely different from sherry's old-fashioned sticky image) are pale Fino and, even lighter, Manzanilla. These are only 15 % alcohol and can be drunk just like any other dry white wine. **Madeira** comes from the Atlantic island of the same name and manages to be both rich and tangy. Most unusually, it can last forever in an opened bottle.

Sweet

Sweet wines can be made in many ways. The sweetness can be the result of stopping fermentation before all the sugar has been converted into alcohol (see pp. 10–11), adding sweet grape concentrate (if cheap), drying grapes to concentrate the sugar, picking frozen grapes (Icewine) and leaving behind the ice, or fermenting grapes that have been concentrated by a strange fungus called botrytis, or 'noble rot'. Sweet wines may currently be unfashionable, but there is nothing inherently bad about a little bit of sugar in a wine, and some of the world's finest wines are sweet. It is really all a question of balance. If there is enough acid in the wine to counterbalance that sweetness, it won't taste at all cloying.

'Wholemeal'

Other special sorts of wine are defined by how they are made. Wine that is certified **organic** is made from vines treated with a minimum of agrochemicals. **Biodynamic** vine growing is even more demanding and involves administering homeopathic doses of strange-sounding natural composts and preparations according to phases of the moon. It sounds completely crazy but results in some pretty exciting wine – and notably healthy-looking vineyards, perhaps because of the extreme vine-by-vine care needed.

One popular current craze is for so-called **natural** wine. There is a distinct camaraderie between producers of vaguely organically grown grapes that are subjected to minimal treatments in the winery – and sometimes, most unusually, absolutely no addition of sulphur, the widespread fruit antioxidant and antiseptic that has been used since Roman times. There are currently no rules governing natural wines, so quality varies enormously.

In practice, most wine producers have been cutting down substantially on the chemicals that were added – far too aggressively – to vines and wines in the decades immediately after the Second World War. I for one would like to see mandatory ingredient-labelling applied to wine as it is to food.

In general I am suspicious of wines marketed on the basis of being organic, biodynamic or natural, but there are certainly very good examples of all of them. I don't think organic wines necessarily taste very different from the norm, while I think I can sometimes taste an extra vitality and energy in biodynamic wines. Occasionally, natural wines can be all too obvious – refermenting, cidery or even slightly redolent of hamster cages – but they are getting better all the time.

Get to know your local independent
wine retailer.

•

You only really need one shape and size
of wine glass, whatever the colour of the
wine, and even champagne and stronger
fortified wines can be enjoyed in your
all-purpose wine glass.

•

There are no rights or wrongs in wine
appreciation. I can explain how to get the most
out of a glass of wine, but it's up to you, not
your supposed 'wine expert' friend, to decide
whether you like it or not.

•

Try not to fill a glass more than half full,
so that you can swirl the wine round and
really enjoy the all-important aromas.

•

Wine comes in cases not crates.
It's a corkscrew, not an 'opener'.

•

Some very good wine is now sealed with screwcaps because producers (and consumers) have become fed up with the taint associated with poorly treated cork.

•

There are some fabulous sweet wines – don't discount them. Top-quality sweet white bordeaux (Sauternes, Barsac) is far better value than its red counterpart.

•

Some of the best-value wines in the world are those that have been unfashionable, such as all but the most celebrated sherries and ports.

•

Temperature matters. Too cold and the wine won't taste of anything; too hot and it'll taste muddy.

•

Colour doesn't matter as much as weight when matching wines and food.

•

How To Handle Wine

Why temperature matters

The most important thing about a glass of wine is, of course, the wine itself. As I've outlined (pp. 48–9), the glass plays a part, but even more important is the temperature at which the wine is served. You can make a wine taste much better, and much worse, by adjusting its temperature.

The warmer a wine is, up to about 20 °C/68 °F, the more molecules are given off and the more aroma it will have. Similarly, the cooler it is, the less smelly it will seem. When I was a student and a good half of all wines sold were horribly full of chemicals, it made sense to chill bad white plonk so savagely you couldn't smell anything. But if you chill white wines too enthusiastically, you might deprive yourself of their single biggest attribute: aroma. Certain grape varieties, such as Sauvignon Blanc and Riesling, are more aromatic than others, so you can afford to chill them a little more than, say, Chardonnay, Pinot Blanc and Pinot Gris, which are intrinsically not particularly smelly.

Another factor is how much body a wine has. The fuller the wine, the more the aroma molecules have to struggle to leave the surface of the wine. So full-bodied whites such as hefty Chardonnays and white Rhône-ish wines need to have their expressiveness encouraged by being served a bit warmer than light-bodied whites such as Riesling, Muscadet, or anything less than 13 % alcohol. This factor works for red wines, too. Light-bodied reds such as Beaujolais, Lambrusco, and the host of lower-alcohol reds now being made in various corners of the world take quite kindly to being served chilled at about 12 °C/54 °F.

The reason many full-bodied reds taste all wrong when they are served too cold is that the chewy tannins so prevalent in young reds (they soften with time) are accentuated at low temperatures. If you want to drink a young red wine that is relatively high in tannin, you can flatter it, making the tannins less obvious, by serving it at a fairly high temperature. Though don't let it get more than 20 °C/68 °F, when the precious aroma starts to become volatile and stewed and all those complex flavours begin to boil off.

In practice, the ideal serving temperature for white burgundies, which are made from Chardonnay and are often full-bodied, is about 15 °C/60 °F, remarkably close to the ideal serving temperature for red burgundies, which are made from Pinot Noir and are often relatively light-bodied wines.

How to chill and warm wine

The simplest way to chill a bottle is to put it into a fridge for a few hours. Be careful of leaving wine in a fridge for more than a few days: long-term storage in a fridge can rob a wine of some of its life and flavour. On the other hand, if I need to chill a bottle in a hurry I have no qualms about putting it into the freezer for up to an hour. But be very careful of leaving a bottle at sub-zero temperatures for any longer than this, because wine freezes and expands at about minus x °C, where 2x is the alcoholic strength of the wine, and the ice formed can push the cork out of the bottleneck. An alternative is to use one of those cooling sleeves that you freeze in the freezer or, generally quicker, to use a good old-fashioned ice bucket. Many people, even professionals, stuff the ice bucket with ice cubes, but it is much more effective to use a mixture of water and ice cubes, because then every bit of the surface of the bottle is in contact with the cooling agent. You do have to deal with the drips, though. If I have a glass of relatively ordinary wine already poured that I want to chill in a hurry, I have been known to add an ice cube, so long as it's a clean, neutral ice cube.

If you need to warm a wine, it's usually enough to leave

the bottle at room temperature for an hour or so. But if you need to warm it in a hurry, you could nurse the bottle and try to transmit your body heat, or pour its contents into a clean jug or decanter that has been rinsed with hot water and then swirl it around a bit. Or, even more effective, you could pour the wine into a glass and then warm the glass in your hands.

Once you have got your bottle to the right temperature, in hot weather, or in hot rooms, it can be very helpful to keep the opened bottle in one of those vacuum bottle coolers designed to maintain temperatures.

When to open the bottle – and whether to decant

For many people, opening a bottle of wine is a religious sacrament. They have evolved arcane rules about how long different sorts of wine need to 'breathe' before being served. Like many wine scientists, I am sceptical that much can happen to the contents of a bottle of wine via the small surface area in a bottleneck, but it is certainly true that exposure to air can have a massive effect on a wine. Too much aeration of a really old, frail wine can destroy it. On the other hand, judicious aeration of a young wine can mimic the ageing process to a certain extent. For instance, a very tannic, astringent young red, and even a tight, introvert, uncommunicative young white (particularly white burgundy), can seem much more approachable after being exposed to air for an hour or two, or even longer for some young reds such as Barolo and some very smart red bordeaux in which tannins and perfumes play an important part. The most effective way of exposing such wines to air is to decant them. The word 'decant' may sound rather pompous and off-putting, but all it involves is pouring the contents of the wine from the bottle into a clean container – ideally made of neutral glass. A glass jug would do, but wine decanters have generally been designed to hold the contents of a 75 cl bottle in such a way that the surface area of the wine is big enough to allow lots of interaction between the wine and air. You can even find special decanters for magnums, which are double-size bottles containing 150 cl of wine. In my experience, junk shops are awash with often relatively inexpensive decanters. Pouring the wine vigorously into the decanter helps to aerate it (as does simply swirling any wine poured into a glass).

Another reason for decanting is to separate the wine from any sediment that may have formed in it, as it not only looks rather unappetising, it can taste bitter. An inexpensive wine that has been aggressively clarified before bottling (by filtration, for example) is highly unlikely to have any deposit in the bottle. But as the various compounds in less industrial wine, particularly tannins and pigments, interact with each other, they precipitate sediment, which can sometimes stick to the inside of the bottle but usually falls to the bottom of an upright bottle. To separate the wine from this sediment most effectively it helps to stand the bottle upright for an hour or so and then pour the wine off the sediment against a bright light, either a carefully placed candle or a strong light source.

If you are planning to serve several wines and want to minimize the likelihood of confusion, you could do what's called 'double decanting'. This involves pouring the wine off any deposit into a jug, rinsing the bottle carefully and pouring the sediment-free wine back into the clean bottle, exposing it to as much air as possible along the way.

Wine leftovers

Because prolonged exposure to air–more than a week or so–can rob even young wines of their fruit, it makes sense to keep leftover wine in contact with as little air as possible, either by squirting some neutral gas into the space left between the wine and stopper in an open bottle (you can buy the necessary canisters for not very much) or by decanting sturdy wines into a smaller bottle. I have not had much luck with those things that are supposed to suck air out of an opened bottle, creating a vacuum.

Because heat speeds up reactions, you can slow the deterioration of wine in an opened bottle by storing it in the fridge. Just remember to bring red wines out in good time before serving.

Coravin

For those who cannot finish a whole 75 cl bottle at a time, there's a new bit of gear that would suit the serious wine geek, invented by Greg Lambrecht, a wine-loving American medical scientist frustrated by the mismatch between his teetotal wife and how much wine a standard bottle contains. The Coravin, which costs about £270, extracts as much or as little wine as you care to consume from a bottle through a tube so thin that the cork reseals itself, and the space left in the bottle by the extracted wine is filled with neutral gas – repelling the oxygen that can ruin a wine if present in any sizeable volume.

Which wines need time?

I know we're always being told that wine improves with age, but that applies to probably less than 10 % of all the wine made today. Most of it – especially rosé and the great majority of whites, but even the red versions of the basic brands and blends, those selling for the lowest prices in the mass market – is made to be drunk within a year of it being bottled. It is only the grandest, most expensive wines – particularly those from France and Italy – that are specifically designed to be stored for many years or even decades after they are put on the market. And even these wines can go over the hill, especially since people tend to sit on their finest wines so long, waiting for ever for an occasion or person special enough to open them for. But most of the world's more interesting wines, the ones referred to in this book, have the ability to gain interest and complexity with a bit of time in the bottle (see overleaf).

At its simplest, wines capable of some bottle development can be a bit shocked by the process of bottling and need a month or three afterwards before becoming expressive again. Young whites can seem a bit too tart in their first few months, and young reds can often be too astringent and tannic in the early years.

As a very general rule, the more expensive a wine within a certain category, the longer it is worth ageing. (This is why it doesn't necessarily make sense to choose the dearest bottle in a shop to drink straightaway.) The obvious exception to this is Condrieu, the quintessential full-bodied white made in the northern Rhône from the Viognier grape, which is never cheap but is rarely worth ageing more than a few years.

On the other hand, in my experience of all but the most expert consumers, once someone decides a bottle is worth keeping, they are far too reluctant to open it, so the bottle sits and sits – often in unsuitable conditions (see p. 66) – until it is well past its best-by date. Because of this, and because many people who buy cheap wine don't realize it is best drunk young, I suspect more wine is drunk too late than too early.

How long to keep wine

Here I suggest the ages at which good examples of various sorts of wine should best be drunk–although of course the very finest examples can usually last longer than indicated.

Still whites
- **plonk** up to a year, but ideally no more than a few months
- **Pinot Grigio** up to 2 years
- **Viognier, Condrieu** up to 2 years
- **Sauvignon Blanc, Sancerre, Pouilly-Fumé** 1–2 years
- **Vinho Verde, Albariño, other Galician whites** 1–2 years
- **Muscat** 1–3 years
- **Rhône-ish whites** 2–5 years
- **Gewürztraminer** 2–6 years
- **Chenin Blanc** 2–10 years
- **Chardonnay, white burgundy** 2–10 years
- **Chablis** 2–12 years
- **Semillon** 3–10 years
- **Riesling** 3–15 years
- **Botrytised sweet wines** 5–20 years

Pink wines
Almost all of these are best drunk at 1–2 years, many of them as young as possible

Reds
- **plonk** up to a year
- **Beaujolais and other Gamay-based wines** 1–5 years

- **Zinfandel/Primitivo** 2–12 years
- **Pinot Noir, red burgundy** 2–15 years
- **Sangiovese, Chianti and Chianti Classico, Brunello di Montalcino** 3–12 years
- **Douro and other Portuguese reds** 4–12 years
- **Grenache/Garnacha, southern Rhône reds** 4–15 years
- **Cabernet Franc, Bourgeuil, Chinon** 4–16 years
- **non-plonk Merlot, right-bank bordeaux** 4–18 years
- **Tempranillo, Rioja, Ribera del Duero** 4–20 years
- **Shiraz/Syrah, northern Rhône reds** 5–25 years
- **non-plonk Cabernet Sauvignon, left-bank bordeaux** 5–25 years
- **Nebbiolo, Barolo, Barbaresco** 10–30 years

Sparkling wine

- **Prosecco, Asti, Moscato, Spumante** as young as possible
- **Cava** 1–2 years
- **crémants** 1–2 years
- **non-vintage champagne** 1–5 years
- **vintage champagne** 2–10 years

Strong, fortified wine

Most of these are released when they are ready to drink. The principal exceptions are below.

- **single-quinta vintage port** 2–20 years
- **vintage port** 15–40 years

How to store wine

It's no good keeping wine in any old store cupboard. And it's an especially bad idea, whatever kitchen designers may suggest, to store wine in a room where the temperature fluctuates as often as it does in most kitchens. Wine is a fragile living thing that needs favourable storage conditions.

They are listed below in declining order of importance:

Temperature should be low: 13 °C/55 °F is ideal, but anywhere between 10 °C/50 °F and 20 °C/68 °F will do, with the proviso that the warmer the storage temperature, the faster the wine will age. The temperature should also be as constant as possible; wine doesn't like dramatic changes.

Light is bad for wine, especially sparkling wine.

Strong smells should be avoided; they might taint the wine.

Humidity should ideally be around 75% relative humidity. If the atmosphere is too dry, corks can start to dry out, shrivel and let in air. If the atmosphere is too humid, the wine will be fine but labels may become mouldy.

All of this means that it can be quite difficult to find a suitable space. A proper cellar is ideal, or a cupboard in a rarely used bedroom might be a reasonable alternative. Garden sheds run the risk of the wine's freezing. A company called Spiral Cellars can install a series of specially shaped breeze blocks that become a spiral staircase with open compartments for bottles leading off it. I had one put in our garden but tree roots punctured the all-important rubber bag around it so that it became far too damp. Many people find the safest, but by no means the cheapest nor most convenient, option is to store wine with commercial specialists. You are generally charged per case or part-case per year and incur charges every time you move wine in or out, but such specialists are good at keeping records of your distant cellar.

Remember that Grape

Grape names – a shortcut to wine knowledge

Something revolutionary happened in the second half of the last century. Many wineries began to label their bottles not with the name of the village or region in which they were produced (Chablis, for instance) but as 'varietals', with the name of the grape variety they were mainly made from (so Chardonnay might be on the label instead of Chablis). The idea was that producers making wine outside those places that had built up reputations over centuries could now communicate to the consumer how their wines were likely to taste – so it made life much easier for producers outside Europe in the so-called New World (an expression that always sounds a bit patronizing to me). But it has also made life much, much easier for wine drinkers. Instead of having to memorize a wine atlas, all they had to do was get to grips with a handful of grape names.

The most famous grapes are profiled here. In the mid 1990s it looked as though all the world's vineyards were being turned over to this handful of vine varieties, but the great new trend is for more obscure, local ones – sometimes called 'heritage varieties'. By 2012, when with co-authors José Vouillamoz and Julia Harding I published a guide to all the grapes we could find being used to make wine commercially, we were able to call it *Wine Grapes: A Complete Guide to 1,368 Vine Varieties Including Their Origins and Flavours*.

MOST COMMON WHITE WINE GRAPES
Chardonnay

Chardonnay is the world's most planted white wine grape, grown virtually everywhere wine is produced. But its home is Burgundy, where it is responsible for virtually all the region's whites. It is blissfully easy to grow and turn into wine and is one of the most versatile grapes in the world, being, for example, the Champagne region's pale-skinned grape while also responsible for the world's most expensive dry whites such as Le Montrachet, as well as for a host of vaguely broad, full-bodied whites at just about every price point. While few inexpensive Chardonnays can be accused of an excess of flavour, they have a great affinity for oak, so some of them can be lightly toasty, even very slightly sweet.

Suggested taste test: Compare a southern-hemisphere Chardonnay (which may well have been aged either in a barrel or with some oak chips to give it an oaky flavour) with a basic Chablis from the far north of Burgundy (typically with no oak). Notice the light sweetness and toastiness of the oak, and see how 'full-bodied' the former is–how unlike water–and how much more acid the Chablis is (although in hotter wine regions winemakers often add acid to compensate for very ripe grapes with low natural acidity).

Sauvignon Blanc

This, the raw material for Loire whites like Sancerre and Pouilly-Fumé and bedrock of the New Zealand wine industry, has become increasingly popular, threatening the dominance of Chardonnay. Whereas Chardonnay is perhaps broad and smudgy, Sauvignon Blanc is sharp, tart and zesty–more like a sword in the direct way it hits the senses. A typical Kiwi example smells pungently of things green such as green leaves, nettles, grass and, as it ages, canned asparagus. A classic example from the upper reaches of the Loire, on the other hand, can be redolent of something more mineral than vegetable: stones, wet chalk, struck matches, something high toned. In very general terms, as is so often the case, French examples are usually much drier than non-French, with New Zealand examples often off-dry. Its piercing aroma is Sauvignon Blanc's strongest suit, but if the grapes get too ripe they can lose that characteristic smell, so the best wines come from areas that are not too warm.

Suggested taste test: Compare a Marlborough (New Zealand) Sauvignon Blanc (as young as possible) with a Sancerre or a white Touraine (which will be made from Sauvignon). Notice the difference in flavours and sugar levels (the Kiwi version being distinctly sweeter under the acidity). Both wines should be relatively high in acidity, because both are made a long way from the equator, which means that summers are not too hot.

Riesling

Riesling is pronounced 'Reeceling' and is one of those funny grapes adored by many professionals but disliked by many consumers. We admire Riesling because, much more than Sauvignon Blanc, its wines can continue to develop and improve in bottle for years, sometimes decades. Longevity is a sign of quality in a wine. We like Riesling because it can have a great deal of flavour without being particularly alcoholic, and, unlike with Sauvignon Blanc and most Chardonnay, its wines vary enormously according to where it is planted. There is often a certain floweriness to how it smells, but, planted on grey or blue slate in the Mosel valley in Germany, it positively tingles with nervous energy, while wines grown just a few miles downstream on red slate are richer and spicier, though always with the framework and spine that characterizes this noble variety. The problem with Riesling is that, unlike Chardonnay or Pinot Gris/Grigio, it has a lot of flavour, and it is perhaps not surprising that that flavour is too much for some tasters. The other problem with Riesling's image is that a significant proportion of Rieslings have a bit of sweetness, and in today's wine-drinking culture sweetness is not viewed as a virtue. Riesling is not grown nearly as widely as Chardonnay and Sauvignon, yet it is a speciality not just of Germany but also of the three As: Alsace, Austria and Australia (especially in the Clare and Eden Valleys).

Suggested taste test: Compare a Riesling from the Mosel, with between 8 and 10 % alcohol, with one from Australia, which will be closer to 13 %. The Australian will almost certainly be bone dry, but see if you can sense the sweetness and lightness of body of the German example. The lower the alcohol, the more of the natural grape sugar will be left, unfermented, in the wine.

Pinot Gris/Grigio

Pinot Gris/Grigio (Grauburgunder in German) is usually white. This 'grey' (*gris* in French and *grigio* in Italian) mutation of Pinot Noir has pink skins that don't have enough colour in them to make a red wine, although if the winemaker leaves the juice in contact with the skins for a while a pale pink wine may result. The best examples, typically from Alsace and from Friuli, in north-east Italy, have an attractively heady perfume and weight about them that hints at some of the qualities of Pinot Noir, while the most basic examples of Pinot Grigio seem to have hardly any flavour at all – which is probably because the wine has, rather mysteriously, become so popular that yields have ballooned and the blend may have been (quite legally) stretched by the addition of up to 15 % of a cheap, neutral grape such as Trebbiano. The pale-green-skinned mutation is 'white' rather than grey, and called **Pinot Blanc/Bianco** (Weissburgunder in German). The wines it produces are like plump, slightly simple Chardonnays, or Pinot Gris without the perfume. Some of the best examples come from German-speaking countries.

Suggested taste test: Compare an Alsace Pinot Gris with an inexpensive supermarket Pinot Grigio. See whether you can identify any common characteristic. The Alsace one is likely to have much more flavour and body.

MOST COMMON RED WINE GRAPES
Cabernet Sauvignon

Cabernet Sauvignon is regarded as the gold-standard grape for red wines designed to age. It's the one primarily responsible for the most famous red bordeaux, such as Château Lafite and Château Latour in the Médoc, on the so-called left bank of the Gironde estuary. It has particularly small, thick-skinned, blueish grapes, so when young the wines tend to be high in tannins and colour. This vine variety takes a long while to ripen, and it's a waste of time planting it somewhere cool. Even parts of Bordeaux can be better suited to its earlier-maturing blending partners and relatives Merlot (see below) and **Cabernet Franc,** the latter being slightly lighter and leafier than Cabernet Sauvignon. In Bordeaux Cabernet Sauvignon can be a little tough and skinny, and it has generally been planted alongside the earlier-ripening and fleshier Merlot as insurance against a poor flowering or a failure in the Cabernet to reach full ripeness. But in its other great hotspot, the Napa Valley, the climate is generally warm enough to produce positively velvety Cabernet Sauvignon, so blending is more of an optional extra. Because it is associated with some of the world's most classic sorts of wine, Cabernet Sauvignon has been planted more or less everywhere it stands a chance of ripening. Its very distinctive imprint of blackcurrant and cedar are highly recognizable all over the globe, even in some Italian wines in which it is only a minor (and sometimes illegal) ingredient.

Suggested taste test: Compare a red Médoc or Graves carrying the name of a château on the label – a wine below

£20/$30 would be fine – and a Chilean Cabernet Sauvignon of more or less the same price and age. Notice how much riper and sweeter the Chilean tastes, thanks to all the extra sunshine enjoyed in Chile. Both wines are likely to have been aged in oak barrels, but nowadays winemakers deliberately avoid any overt oakiness.

Merlot

Merlot is part of the same big vine family of south-west France as the Cabernet Sauvignon and Cabernet Franc, but it differs from them in how much softer and fruitier its wines are. The vine ripens earlier so can be planted in cooler places, such as its home in St-Émilion and Pomerol on the right bank of the Gironde. Because it is so much easier to ripen than Cabernet Sauvignon, it is more widely planted – especially in the extensive Bordeaux region. The wines are naturally sweet and plummy and definitely softer and earlier maturing than Cabernet-dominated wines. One of Merlot's big jobs is to add flesh to the frame of Cabernet in blends, but varietal Merlots are produced all over the world.

Suggested taste test: Compare the 'petit château' (see p. 44) from the Médoc or Graves used in the Cabernet Sauvignon taste test (whose main grape will almost certainly be Cabernet Sauvignon) with one at about the same price whose appellation is simply Bordeaux (which is almost certainly made mainly from Merlot). Notice how much lighter, softer and rounder is the latter.

Pinot Noir

This, the red burgundy grape, has a fair claim to be the current darling of the wine world. While Cabernet Sauvignon is reliable, Pinot Noir is tantalizingly variable. When it's good, it's delicious, but it is fragile and much lighter than Cabernet. The grape skins are a lot thinner, so the grapes are more susceptible to rot and disease, and the resulting wines are paler and usually less tannic or chewy. Pinot Noir is typically fruity, sometimes a little sweet, tasting variously of raspberries, cherries, violets, mushrooms and autumnal undergrowth. Although it is relatively finicky, it has attracted the interest of producers and consumers all over the world, but, because it is early-ripening, it needs a fairly cool climate for the growing season to be long enough for the grapes to develop interesting flavours. Burgundy is its birthplace, but Pinot Noir is also the most important red wine grape of Champagne, Alsace, Germany, New Zealand and Oregon. Some interesting examples are now being made in the coolest parts of California, Chile and Australia, and ambitious Pinotphiles are making progress from Canada to South Africa.

Suggested taste test: Red burgundy is made in such small quantities that it is never cheap. Comparing it with a non-French Pinot Noir should demonstrate similar phenomena to the taste test suggested for Sauvignon Blanc. Perhaps more educational in the long run would be to compare one of the more affordable and accessible red burgundies, one labelled simply 'Bourgogne' (French for Burgundy) with a good quality Beaujolais, made from the Gamay grape (see p. 80 for a list of names of the Beaujolais crus, generally the finest wines of the region). Notice how the Gamay is higher in acid and even lower in tannin than Pinot Noir, with more open, obvious fruitiness and a sort of juiciness. Gamay is typically much earlier maturing than Pinot Noir.

Syrah/Shiraz

Shiraz is the Australian name for the grape known as Syrah in its homeland, the northern Rhône valley, whose most famous wines are Hermitage and Côte Rôtie. Much more of it is now planted in Australia than in the northern Rhône, and in hot regions such as Barossa Valley and McLaren Vale it produces rich, dark, dense, sweetish, chocolatey and often rather medicinal essences. The northern Rhône style is quite different, even if Hermitage at least is still dense: bone dry, haunting, with notes of black pepper and leather, but fairly reserved initially. Nowadays many a New World, even Australian, producer chooses to try to emulate the transparency of a Côte Rôtie and signals that intention by calling the wine Syrah rather than Shiraz (although the name Syrah has always been favoured by American producers, whose wines tend to split the difference between the two styles). Since the 1990s Syrah/Shiraz has become an increasingly popular choice with growers all over the world, especially in South Africa and the Languedoc.

Suggested taste test: Compare a Shiraz, preferably Australian, with a Syrah – either an Australian or South African so labelled. Notice how much more delicate the latter is.

Tempranillo

The tobacco-leaf-scented Tempranillo is the most highly regarded red wine grape in Spain, being the main ingredient in Rioja, Ribera del Duero and a host of other Spanish reds. Because Spain has such low rainfall, and until recently had hardly any irrigation, vines are traditionally very widely spaced (which explains why the areas planted with Tempranillo and Spain's workhorse white grape Airén feature so high up the list of the world's most planted wine grapes). Furthermore, Spanish growers have been planting like crazy, with Tempranillo usually the grape of choice because, until recently, they tended to value it much more highly than their native Garnacha – known as Grenache in France. (Garnacha is juicier and lighter than Tempranillo, so was perhaps seen as less serious.) Portugal, where it is also known as Tinta Roriz and Aragonez, is the only other country in which Tempranillo is relatively important.

Suggested taste test: Compare wines from modernist Rioja bodegas such as Artadi, Contador, Finca Allende or Roda with traditional examples from the likes of CVNE, La Rioja Alta, López de Heredia or Muga. They will give you an idea of how Tempranillo tastes, but will also show you the contrasting effects of ageing wine for a shorter time in young, sometimes French, oak (the first group) and a longer time in old American oak, traditional in the region (the second).

Nebbiolo

This might be called the Pinot Noir of Italy, so tantalizingly difficult is it to grow outside its homeland in Piemonte, north-west Italy. Its heady perfume of tar, woodsmoke and roses is typically combined with an unusual combination of pale colour and quite notable tannins. At its best, in the greatest Barolo and Barbaresco, it can yield exceptionally long-lived wines. But it is so late ripening that it demands the most favourable vineyard sites. Less propitious land in Piemonte is more likely to be planted with the lively, sour-cherry **Barbera** and the softer, earlier-maturing **Dolcetto** – both of these being local specialities.

Suggested taste test: Simply get your hands on an affordable and accessible example of this great grape – perhaps a Nebbiolo d'Alba or Langhe Nebbiolo – and pray you don't fall too madly in love with it, as a cellar full of Barolo is going to cost you a lot of money.

Sangiovese

This Central Italian grape is much more widely planted than Nebbiolo, and very downmarket examples exist. But when the plant material is carefully selected and yields are restricted, it can make wines that taste like the very essence of Tuscany. Brunello di Montalcino, from the warm south of the region, is the most ambitious and longest-lived. Chianti Classico, from the cooler hills of central Tuscany, can be rather more refined. The wines typically have a distinctly agricultural but by no means unpleasant whiff.

Suggested taste test: Arm yourself with an inexpensive varietal Sangiovese (one labelled principally with the grape name), perhaps from Romagna, and a Chianti Classico ('Classico' means it's from the heartland of the Chianti region, as opposed to one labelled simply Chianti) that will be made mainly from good-quality Sangiovese. Both should have notable acidity and tanginess, but notice how much more concentrated the Chianti Classico is, both in terms of colour and depth of flavour. Sangiovese isn't smart and suave. It has a certain farmyard quality to it – but an attractive one in the right hands. Think Tuscan hills.

The ten most planted grape varieties

The most recent set of reliable global statistics date from 2010 and are based on the area of vineyards rather than the actual number of vines.

1. **Cabernet Sauvignon**

2. **Merlot**

3. **Airén***

4. **Tempranillo**

5. **Chardonnay**

6. **Syrah/Shiraz**

7. **Grenache/Garnacha**

8. **Sauvignon Blanc**

9. **Trebbiano Toscano**

10. **Pinot Noir**

* The basic white wine grape of the plains of La Mancha – much used for Spanish brandy.

Wine Regions You Need to Know About – A Cheat Sheet

This book is designed to equip you with the essentials. There is of course much, much more to discover, and you should feel absolutely free to explore the wonderful world of wine in more detail. You can read more books, go online (see p. 112 for suggestions), or even visit these magnificent regions which, more often than not, lend themselves to wonderful holidays. For now, here's the skinny on the main wine regions across the world.

(Main grape varieties, red (R) and white (W), are listed in declining order of importance according to the most recent reliable vineyard censuses.)

FRANCE

France competes with Italy as the world's most prolific wine producer, and it is the birthplace of the systematic geographical naming of wines, based on the appellation system. In France, this is expressed as 'Appellation d'Origine Contrôlée', or AOC. (A small problem is that the EU is currently revising its quality designation system, so some labels now say 'AOP' (P for 'Protegée')–grrr.) But things are changing. A new generation of iconoclasts are deliberately deciding to sell their wines without any more geographical indication than 'Vin de France'. And an increasing proportion of them are made as 'natural wine', with minimal additions.

Bordeaux [R: Merlot, Cabernet Sauvignon, Cabernet Franc W: Sauvignon Blanc, Sémillon] Individual producers in the south-western region are known as 'châteaux' (French for 'castles'), even if the wine is made in a shed. Bordeaux has some of the most expensive wines in the world, notably the 'first growths', so called after a classification arranged the best-known châteaux into five divisions, football-style, way back in 1855. These are the sorts of wines traded around the world as investments, and prices are therefore often inflated by speculators. But in fact the region is so big that far more prevalent are modest farmers (petits châteaux), who are finding life very difficult at the moment because their production costs are not so much less than those of the classified growths and yet their prices are relatively low. The result is that Bordeaux can offer some of the worst and best red wine value in the world. Wines produced in the Médoc and Graves on the left bank of the Gironde estuary on which the city of Bordeaux is sited are dry, long-lived and dominated by Cabernet Sauvignon, while those made on the right bank in St-Émilion and Pomerol, and between the two rivers ('Entre-Deux-Mers') that feed into the Gironde, are fruitier and dominated by Merlot.

Other vineyards in south-west France, such as those of the **Dordogne**, **Bergerac** and **Cahors**, tend to grow grape varieties that are part of the greater Bordeaux family.

Burgundy [R: Pinot Noir W: Chardonnay] Individual grower-winemakers in this eastern region are known as 'domaines' (as distinct from 'negociants', or merchants, who make wine from grapes bought from others). The east-facing limestone golden slope, the Côte d'Or, has all the most famous Burgundy vineyards but produces less than a tenth as much wine as Bordeaux. More than two thirds of it is red, from a patchwork of tiny vineyards, each with their own name and status, carefully delineated since the Middle Ages, with twenty or so Grands Crus at the top of the tree, then Premiers Crus, then village wines – some of them from named vineyards, so-called 'lieux-dits', a notch below Premier Cru status. At the bottom of the tree are the regional appellations with the word 'Bourgogne' (French for Burgundy) in the name. Some of the few bargains available in Burgundy are Bourgognes from top growers. Many villages have appended the name of their most famous vineyard to their name, fuelled for example by Gevrey's pride in its Chambertin vineyard and Chambolle's in the incomparable Musigny vineyard. The northern half of the Côte d'Or, the Côte de Nuits (named after the town of Nuits-St-Georges), is devoted almost exclusively to red wine.

The same naming system applies to white burgundy, with the most famous white-wine villages – Puligny-Montrachet, Chassagne-Montrachet and Meursault – being concentrated in the south of the southern half of the Côte d'Or, the Côte de Beaune. None of these wines are cheap. These geographically precise Chardonnays are all aged in oak. There have recently been mysterious and worrying problems with some of the wines turning brown and losing fruit prematurely. In the far north of greater Burgundy is Chablis – made from Chardonnay at its steeliest and, usually, without oak. The best are slow-burning bargains.

Beaujolais/Mâconnais [R: Gamay W: Chardonnay] South of the Côte d'Or and its southern coda the Côte Chalonnaise are these two contiguous regions. The Chardonnays, made mainly in the Mâconnais, are much cheaper, less serious, fruitier and earlier maturing than white wines made further north, but they are recognizably related to them. The reds are made from Gamay, a grape quite different from that used for more northerly burgundy, and are designed to be particularly refreshing – sometimes served cool (it is not a sin to serve red wine cool) and often drunk very young. The best wines from the Beaujolais 'crus' – Regnié, Chiroubles, Chénas, St-Amour, Fleurie, Brouilly, Côte de Brouilly, Juliénas, Morgon and Moulin-à-Vent, in ascending general level of body and ageability – rarely carry the word 'Beaujolais' on the label.

Champagne [R:Pinot Meunier, Pinot Noir W: Chardonnay] Only fizz made of grapes grown in the region next to Disneyland to the east of Paris may call itself champagne; the rest is sparkling wine. Almost all of the wine is white, made from grapes of both colours pressed so gently that no pigments remain in the finished wine, though an increasing proportion is tinted pink by added still red wine. Most champagne is a blend of several vintages (usually with one dominant) and is sold as a non-vintage (or 'NV') wine. A small proportion is made from a single year and is called vintage champagne. And then there are the prestige or de luxe champagnes, such as Cristal and Dom Pérignon, priced to appeal to the status seeker. See p. 53 for how these base wines are made fizzy.

Northern Rhône [R: Syrah W: Viognier, Marsanne, Roussanne] Transparent red from the steep slopes of the Côte Rôtie contrasts with the denser, firmer stuff from the relatively small area of the hill of Hermitage, an hour's drive south. St-Joseph, Crozes-Hermitage and Cornas are more affordable. The first two, and Hermitage, come in white versions too, while the most famous white of the northern Rhône, Condrieu, is made from the perfumed Viognier grape, grown on slopes just south of Côte Rôtie. All production is small scale, but very local and historic.

Southern Rhône [R: Grenache, Syrah W: Grenache Blanc, Vermentino] This is a massive wine region, producing almost as much AOC wine as Bordeaux. Côtes-du-Rhône and the rather superior Côtes-du-Rhône Villages are the quantitatively most important appellations, while the most famous appellation is Châteauneuf-du-Pape, which may well contain a cocktail of local vine varieties. Mourvèdre is the most important of these minor ingredients and is increasingly popular. While most southern Rhône wine is red, there is a fiery pink from Tavel, and some white wine is made in most appellations. The exception to this is Gigondas, which is exclusively red and almost as heady, spicy and potent as the lower-lying Châteauneuf-du-Pape.

Loire [R: Cabernet Franc, Gamay W: Melon de Bourgogne, Chenin Blanc, Sauvignon Blanc] The long river Loire links four distinct and substantial wine regions, and many smaller ones along the way – all of them making wines that are relatively crisp and light. Way upriver are the Central Loire vineyards of Sancerre and Pouilly-Fumé, making very similar wines that are French prototype Sauvignon Blancs (see pp. 68–9); some light reds and pink Pinot Noirs are also produced. Way round the westward bend downriver are the Touraine vineyards around the city of Tours, where a wide variety of whites, dry and sweet, are made from Chenin Blanc in Vouvray and Montlouis and where some breezy, sometimes tart, reds are based mainly on Cabernet Franc – notably Chinon and Bourgeuil. Just downriver of here are the wines of Saumur and Anjou, centred on the cities of Saumur and Angers respectively. Cabernet Franc and Chenin Blanc are the dominant grapes here too, but lighter reds based on Gamay and an array of local grapes can be found throughout this middle section of the Loire.

Around the mouth of the river is the extensive, but currently impoverished because unfashionable, Muscadet wine region. The wines are made from the Melon de Bourgogne grape, whose best wines seem to have a saltiness about them. Muscadet and oysters is a classic combo.

Alsace [R: Pinot Noir W: Riesling, Gewürztraminer, Pinot Blanc, Pinot Gris] This region on the north-eastern French border has been German in its time, and the wines, as in Germany, have long been labelled by grape variety – very un-French. The trend now, however, is to label the wines – mainly white, dry(ish), unoaked, pure and aromatic – with the vineyard name too, notably for the fifty-odd Grands Crus; some growers even refuse to cite any grape, preferring to communicate the essence of place in the bottle instead. Most Alsace whites seem to me to have a vaguely smoky perfume. The red Pinots are getting better all the time.

Languedoc-Roussillon [R: Syrah, Grenache, Carignan, Merlot, Cabernet Sauvignon, Cinsaut W: Chardonnay, Sauvignon Blanc, Muscat, Grenache Blanc] This is a vast wine region, a sweep of vines, mainly dark-skinned varieties, from the Spanish border round to the southern Rhône. It used to make little other than huge quantities of over-produced plonk and strong, sweet Muscats and Grenaches from the hinterland of Perpignan in Roussillon. But from the late twentieth century on, the region has seen a revolution. The least promising vineyards, typically on the fertile plains, have been pulled up, encouraged by subsidies from the EU. Meanwhile, the big producers have been churning out easily saleable inexpensive varietals (hence all that Merlot and Chardonnay) that are usually sold as Pays d'Oc. But more and more great, and generally underpriced, wine is produced by hundreds of small-scale producers, mainly in the hills and labelled with appellations such as (west to east) Fitou, Corbières, Minervois, Faugères and St Chinian, alongside the more general appellation Languedoc. Most of these wines are blends, typically of the first three red wine grapes cited above, often spiced with Cinsaut or Mourvèdre, and they express the local conditions eloquently. The whites used to be a bit heavy, sometimes oaky, but it's not difficult to find really exciting whites now, especially from old vines in the higher reaches of Roussillon. These wines may be labelled Côtes Catalanes. In the Pyrenean foothills, Limoux makes some very respectable sparkling wine. Banyuls, on the coast just north of Spain, makes France's answer to port; the unfortified version is called Collioure.

Jura [R: Poulsard, Pinot Noir, Trousseau W: Chardonnay, Savagnin] This very small region between Burgundy and the alps is famous for Bresse chickens, Comté cheese and vin jaune,

France's answer to dry sherry. But its wines are hugely distinctive and, now, rather fashionable. Alcohol levels are modest, and the whites always tangy and hugely refreshing.

ITALY

Italy has more indigenous grape varieties than any other country. It often makes more wine than France. Although it lacks France's long tradition of fine-wine production, it is making up for it now with a wonderfully titillating range of flavours and styles. Each region has its own personality and grapes. The naming of wines is as anarchic as you would expect. The Italian answer to France's AOC is the DOC (Denominazione di Origine Controllata), but they added a layer above. DOCG is supposedly not just controlled, but guaranteed (the G stands for 'garantita')! Then came a wave of wines just as highly priced but carrying the lowly Vino da Tavola (table wine) designation. Cue chaos. Today many of the wines are simply labelled IGT (Indicazione Geografica Tipica) plus the name of the region or more specific area they come from.

Piemonte [R: Barbera, Dolcetto, Nebbiolo W: Muscat/Moscato, Cortese] Nebbiolo (see p. 75) grown in the Langhe hills south of Turin is responsible for superstars Barolo and Barbaresco, Italy's most revered wines. The best, like the best burgundies, express a single named vineyard. Barbera, often oaked and bitter-cherry-like, is made in much greater quantity, and Dolcetto ('little sweet one') can provide an affordable taste of youthful Piemonte. This is also the home of light grapey fizz such as Asti, the original Moscato before it was hijacked into an international commodity. To the north, at the foot of the **Aosta** valley, which produces some ethereal mountain wines, is another cluster of tantalizing pale Nebbiolo-based reds carrying names such as Gattinara, Ghemme, Lessona Boca and Bramaterra. (Valtellina constitutes another cluster over the border in **Lombardy** just south of the Swiss border, where Nebbiolo is ripened on sun-baked, south-facing alpine foothills.)

Trentino-Alto Adige [R: Teroldego, Lagrein, Pinot Noir W: Chardonnay, Pinot Grigio, Pinot Bianco, Sauvignon Blanc] Trentino is the southern half of this narrow suntrap of a valley, the main traffic artery between Italy and Austria. Many of its vineyards produce base material for sparkling wine, some of the best now called Trento DOC. Teroldego is a bracing local red. Further up the valley is Alto Adige, known as south Tyrol in German (a language that is just as common, in this land of dumplings and dirndls, as Italian). The clear mountain air seems to result in beautifully clear fruit flavours in a wide range of varietally labelled wines, more white than red. Some of the world's best wine co-operatives are to be found here.

Friuli [R: Cabernet Franc, Refosco W: Friulano, Pinot Grigio, Sauvignon Blanc, Pinot Bianco, Ribolla Gialla] Friuli was the first Italian wine region to master modern white-wine production with really fresh flavours. It still makes particularly crystalline varietals and specializes in interesting white blends. Collio and Colli Orientali are the most common DOCs. It is also the birthplace of the new wave of funky, chewy, orangey whites fermented in contact with grape skins and aged not in barrels but in amphorae, a trend that has travelled across the (very casual) border into **Slovenia**'s westernmost wine region, Brda.

Veneto [R: Corvina W: Garganega] This region in the hinterland of Venice was traditionally most famous for Valpolicella and Soave, but nowadays its most famous wine is the hugely successful Prosecco, made in tanks from a grape once called Prosecco but renamed Glera so that Prosecco could be registered as an exclusive (if extensive) geographical region, meaning that no one else could use the term. Soave, of very varying quality, continues, while more and more of the dark-skinned grapes are picked late and then dried to produce the potent (and more lucrative) Amarone della Valpolicella.

Tuscany [R: Sangiovese, Cabernet Sauvignon W: Trebbiano Toscano] Along with Piemonte, Tuscany (Toscana in Italian) is the red-wine heart of Italy. Oceans of tangy Chianti are produced, mainly from Sangiovese, on the atmospheric, cypress-lined hills south of Florence, and the finest come from individual estates in the best, central zone known as Chianti Classico. (All over Italy, Classico refers to an original zone before it has been enlarged, which has generally happened for reasons of commercial expediency.) More concentrated, longer-living and from warmer, more southerly territory is Brunello di Montalcino, Brunello being the name of a local form of Sangiovese. Vino Nobile di Montepulciano is similar but not quite as revered. On the Tuscan coast around Bolgheri is a cluster of ambitious producers who, inspired by the prototype Sassicaia that emerged in the 1970s, make top-quality bordeaux blends. Most Tuscan dry whites are pretty ordinary, typically based on the very neutral Trebbiano Toscano grape (known as Ugni Blanc in France and used mainly for distilling into brandy). The most exciting whites are tawny, tangy, sweet Vin Santo made from dried Malvasia grapes.

Umbria, the landlocked region immediately south of Tuscany, can boast the more interesting dry whites of Orvieto and its own fiery, tough red wine grape Sagrantino, a speciality of the town of Montefalco. Sangiovese is the most common Umbrian grape, however.

Marche [R: Sangiovese, Montepulciano W: Verdicchio] The most famous wine made on the Adriatic coast is white, made from the Verdicchio grape. The best examples can age beautifully, but always have a certain lemony quality. Rosso Conero and Rosso Piceno are the local reds.

Campania [R: Aglianico W: Fiano, Falanghina, Greco] The vineyards around Naples can trace their history back at least to Roman times, and the (relatively full-bodied) wines seem to have a sort of classical nobility to me. The whites have a certain leafy quality, while the reds, of which Taurasi is the finest, are firm, plummy and somehow mineral. Both whites and reds age well.

Puglia [R: Negroamaro, Primitivo (Zinfandel), Nero di Troia, Malvasia Nera W: Bombino Bianco, Minutolo] For decades the relatively flat, baked heel of Italy churned out strong, dark reds that were routinely shipped north to be blended into much more famous wines. This continues today but, after EU subsidies have cleared it of many vineyards, it is forging an identity for its better wines. Most are red, robust and potent, sometimes with some apparent sweetness. Whites are also hefty and may need added acid to keep them fresh. Rosés can be more successful.

Sardinia [R: Cannonau (Grenache), Carignano (Carignan) W: Vermentino] This dry island has enormous potential, which is slowly being realized. Its fragrant dry white Vermentino is now being copied far and wide. Powerful, rich, gunpowdery Carignano del Sulcis, made on the southern tip of Sardinia, is my personal favourite form of Carignan.

Sicily [R: Nero d'Avola, Nerello W: Catarratto] Sicily used to perform the same workhorse function as Puglia, but this often-conquered island is currently one of Italy's most exciting wine regions. The west is dominated by the rather simple Catarratto, once planted in profusion for Marsala, today made mainly for the kitchen. Nero d'Avola, with its sweet cherry fruit, is the red wine grape of western Sicily, while eastern vineyards are more varied. Etna has become a hotspot, producing transparent, exciting wines that seem to whisper their volcanic origins. They are based on Nerello Mascalese and occasionally Nerello Cappuccio grapes. Then there are all sorts of other, often historic little wine areas.

SPAIN

Spain has more land devoted to the vine than any other country – partly because rainfall is so low and irrigation so impractical that vines have to be particularly widely spaced. (France and Italy make far more wine.) Apart from some Bobal, Garnacha and Tempranillo, the baked plains of La Mancha south of Madrid are planted with a sea of Airén, a neutral white grape variety used to make base wine for Spanish brandy and only rarely seen on wine labels. The Spanish answer to France's AOC is DO (Denominación de Origen). While most wine maps in Europe have changed little over the last few decades, Spain seems to be constantly sprouting new DOs, indicating not new plantings but status upgrades of established vineyards. There is massive variety in smallish DOs not detailed below, from lightly fizzy Txakolina wines in the Basque country on the north coast, through Navarra to Somontano in the Pyrenean foothills, and a mass of traditional wine regions on the central Mediterranean coast that are graduating from being merely a source of strapping reds for blending. Even the Canary Islands, way south of mainland Spain, are producing fascinating wines nowadays.

Galicia and Bierzo [R: Garnacha, Mencía W: Albariño, Godello] The green, Atlantic-washed north-west of Spain has become a fashionable source of some of Spain's most refreshing wines. Rías Baixas are fjord-like inlets on the west coast where vines, often on pergolas supported by granite posts, produce marine-scented dry whites, typically labelled Albariño and not unlike the Vinho Verde made on the other side of the Miño/Minho river in Portugal. Ribeiro and Valdeorras (for Puligny-like Godello varietals) also make fine dry white while the steep valleys of Ribeira Sacra yield unusually fresh reds. Bierzo is technically just over the border in León but belongs to the same group of wines created by unusual (slate) soils, local grapes and cooling Atlantic influence. The super-fruity, fresh Mencía is Bierzo's gift to the wine world.

Rioja [R: Tempranillo, Garnacha (Grenache) W: Viura (Macabeo)] Rioja is Spain's historic fine-wine region, given a huge boost in the late nineteenth century when Bordeaux producers, whose European vines had been laid waste by phylloxera, a native American louse unwittingly imported with botanical specimens shipped across the Atlantic, crossed the Pyrenees in search of an alternative source of wine. The tradition was for grapes to be grown by local smallholders, who often made them into wine themselves, and then the wineries, or bodegas, would buy in wine, blend it and age it for many a long year in small American oak barrels, or *barricas*. This made Rioja, most of it pale red and sweetish with the vanilla whiff of American oak, one of the longest-aged wines available – and the tradition was always to sell it only after many years in oak. Most revered were the oldest, those that were at least five years old and qualified as Gran Reservas, with Reservas a lttle lower down the tree, and then Crianza with some oak ageing and Joven all young and fruity. But other sorts of Rioja have emerged recently. Nowadays, the bodegas make the wine them-selves – in a wider variety of styles. More concentrated, darker, younger reds are the result of shorter ageing in French oak. And an increasing number of producers are de-termined to express geography, often single estates or even single vineyards, in their Riojas. Tempranillo (see pp. 74–5) dominates the two subregions in the Atlantic-influenced west of the region, Rioja Alta and Rioja Alavesa in Alava province, but juicier, sweeter Garnacha is the grape of the lower elevation, the Mediterranean-influenced Rioja Baja. About a seventh of the vines have pale skins and make whites, from crisp wines to long-lived, oaked essences.

Ribera del Duero, Rueda and Toro [R: Tempranillo W: Verdejo] The Duero river links these three regions as it flows west on a high plateau towards Portugal, where it becomes the Douro. From the 1980s and especially in the 1990s, encouraged by the price of its twentieth-century superstar Pingus, there was an investment frenzy in the region so that there are now more than 200 bodegas, many of them speculative buildings without many vines. Although the raw ingredients – mainly Tempranillo plus ageing in small oak barrels – are similar, Ribera tastes quite different from Rioja. There's a much deeper colour, and a more precise palate profile, presumably because the elevation and cool nights preserve freshness. The oak in some of them can be a bit intrusive.

Tempranillo, known here as Tinta de Toro, is the dominant grape of Toro, too. Toro is downriver of Ribera and is warmer, producing riper, more alcoholic, positively full-blooded wines. Between these two red wine regions is Rueda, whose crisp, dry whites made from the local Verdejo grape, and sometimes Sauvignon Blanc, are much sought-after in Spain. Again, altitude keeps in the freshness.

Catalunya [R: Garnatxa (Grenache), Cabernet Sauvignon, Merlot, Tempranillo, Carinyena (Carignan) W: Macabeo, Xarello, Parellada] The gastronomically dynamic north-east of the country in the hinterland of Barcelona produces a wide range of different wines. Best-known is Cava, most but not all of it made, in the same painstaking way as champagne (see p. 53), around the Penedès town of Sant Sadurni d'Anoya. Traditionally, Cava is based on the three white wine grapes cited above, but the champagne grapes Chardonnay and Pinot Noir are now making inroads. Quality varies enormously, but there are some very fine Catalan sparkling wines, with some of the most ambitious producers preferring not to use the Cava DO. From obscurity as recently as the 1980s, Priorat has emerged as the region's red-wine superstar (and is the producer of a few hefty whites). Based on ancient, low-yielding Garnacha and Cariñena vines apparently sprouting out of the local dark *licorella* rock, these are concentrated wines that taste as though they have been yielded unwillingly by the warm rock underneath. Montsant next door makes similar but slightly lighter wines. Some of the region's most interesting wines come from higher ground well inland, such as Conca de Barberá, and there are interesting initiatives even further inland in Costers del Segre. Empordà in the Costa Brava makes wines rather like Roussillon just over the border.

Andalucia [W: Palomino Fino, Pedro Ximénez] Although there has recently been some investment in unfortified wines and a revival in the tradition of making sweet Muscats in the hills above the Costa del Sol, notably around Ronda, this is essentially sherry country. The main sherry town is Jerez, and when I started to write about wine in the mid 1970s it felt like the centre of the wine world. But the sherry business has since been shrunk by overproduction, price-cutting and an image problem. All of which is a great shame, since proper sherry is arguably Spain's most distinctive wine. It is made from Palomino Fino grapes grown on chalky land around Jerez and the little whitewashed port of Sanlucar de Barrameda. The resulting wine is aged in old barrels, or butts, traditionally in airy bodegas cooled by Atlantic breezes but nowadays often in more prosaic warehouses with computer-controlled temperature and humidity. Neutral grape spirit is added to the young wine to 'fortify' it, and much of it is kept fresh under a film of yeast that looks like dough and is called 'flor'. The most delicate, palest sherries are Manzanilla and Fino, the former a speciality of Sanlucar de Barrameda and supposedly tasting a little salty from its proximity to the sea. They are only 15 % alcohol, so barely more than many an unfortified wine grown in a hot climate. Amontillado is basically a long-aged Fino. Darker sherries such as Oloroso are aged without flor and can be a bit stronger. Cream sherry is sweetened with grape concentrate, but it's the drier styles we aficionados appreciate – not least because most of them are still ridiculously underpriced. An appreciation of dry sherry has become a sign of connoisseurship nowadays. North-east of the sherry region is the warmer Montilla-Moriles region, which makes similar but softer wines and, most notably, a dentist's nightmare of sweet, sticky treacly wine from the local Pedro Ximénez grape. Montilla-Moriles has traditionally supplied sweetening wine to Jerez.

USA

The US is the world's fourth biggest producer of wine, and, since California produces 90 % of all American wine, California alone can be regarded as a superpower in wine terms. The legacy of Prohibition is that selling wine in the US can be a complex business, hamstrung by factional restrictions. And Americans have been much slower to embrace wine than one might expect of a country made up of immigrants from so many wine-consuming and wine-producing countries. Recently, however, helped by Millennial enthusiasm for the grape, the US at long last overtook France as the world's biggest market for wine. There is no direct equivalent of France's AOC in the US, but there are American Viticultural Areas (AVAs), officially delineated geographical areas, some of them, such as Washington state's Columbia Valley, absolutely vast (11 million acres!) and extremely varied. Others, such as Stag's Leap District in Napa Valley, are much smaller and more homogenous.

California [R: Cabernet Sauvignon, Zinfandel, Merlot, Pinot Noir W: Chardonnay, (French) Colombard, Sauvignon Blanc, Pinot Gris] California is a massive player in the world of wine. The great bulk of the volume is grown in the sun-baked Central Valley and sold with the catch-all appellation California and, often, the name of a well-known brand and/or producer. E & J Gallo dominates production here and is the world's biggest wine producer. (Gallo also has fingers in many a more upmarket pie.) The following, roughly from north to south, are the more interesting regions within California.

Mendocino Folk songs and folksy wines abound in a county where organic techniques took hold much earlier than elsewhere. And in the pine forests of **Anderson Valley** are vineyards cool enough to produce refined sparkling wine and aromatic Rieslings and Gewürztraminer.

Sonoma Sonoma county, north-west of Napa country, prides itself on being 'not Napa' – less glitzy and more homespun. It has some of the coolest vineyards in the state out by the Pacific in the western reaches of the far-too-big **Sonoma Coast** AVA. Pinot Noir and Chardonnay predominate here, as they have long done in the rather warmer **Russian River Valley** inland, whose wines are a little richer. To the north (and still definitely warm and inland) are **Dry Creek Valley,** famous for old-vine Zinfandel, some originally planted by Italian immigrants, and the extensive **Alexander Valley**, where some fine Cabernet Sauvignon is grown.

Napa Napa Valley, a simple farming community in the early 1970s, has become the world's most glamorous wine region. Blessed with a winning combination of natural beauty, reliable sunshine, regular natural temperature control from the Pacific coast to the west, and unlimited capital both from Silicon Valley to the south and myriad successful American businessmen keen to invest their hard-won fortunes in the dream of wine production, it has become a magnet for tourists. At weekends, traffic can move at a snail's pace, but the views, the tasting programmes and the restaurants can make up for it. The closer the vineyards are to the Bay – the more southerly – the cooler they tend to be. So **Carneros**, which straddles the Napa–Sonoma county line, is coolest of all and has been targeted by those making sparkling wine, as well as still Pinot Noir and Chardonnay. Then, very roughly moving north, come the most famous sub-appellations **Stags Leap**, **Oakville**, **Rutherford** and **St Helena**, although such is the power of the Napa Valley name, and the frequency of blending between sub appellations, that they are cited on labels in only a minority of cases. Cabernet Sauvignon dominates plantings and can produce some of its most luscious examples here, often from grapes so ripe that acids and tannins are much lower than in Bordeaux and there is no need to blend in any softening Merlot.

Sierra Foothills The old mining country on the way to the Sierra Nevada no longer grows that much wine but has some particularly old vineyards, especially of Zinfandel, and makes wines with no shortage of folksy character. The terrain is very different from the manicured lawns and statuary of Napa Valley.

South of the Bay Some of California's finest wine and oldest vines are in isolated, and often notably high, pockets in the **Santa Cruz Mountains** between Silicon Valley and the Pacific. The wind tunnel that is Salinas Valley in **Monterey** county just south of here has been farmed for all manner of crops, including grapes, on an industrial scale. A wide variety of grapes are grown here, with perhaps the most interesting wines made from Pinot Noir grown at higher elevations such as **Santa Lucia Highlands**, **Chalone** (note the difference between the Chalone AVA and the brand that is now used much more liberally) and on the pioneering Calera estate in the Mount Harlan AVA.

San Luis Obispo and Santa Barbara Central Coast is California's biggest AVA. It runs 250 miles from San Francisco Bay to just east of Santa Barbara, so the areas described above as South of the Bay are part of it. But, in common parlance, Central Coast is often used to denote the vast sprawl of large commercial vineyards that have been planted south of Monterey in San Luis Obispo and Santa Barbara counties. During the Mission period of early Californian history, San Luis Obispo was regarded as producing the state's finest wines, but viticulture was only revived here, enthusiastically, from the 1980s. In the north of San Luis Obispo county is **Paso Robles,** a relatively warm, sometimes dangerously dry, inland enclave best known for Rhône varieties that has seen massive growth in plantings recently. South of here is the cooler **Edna Valley** AVA, developed by agribusinesses, and the more limited **Arroyo Grande**, where Talley Vineyards is the star.

Santa Barbara county was put on the wine map in 2004 by the movie *Sideways*. Although it's so far south, its topography is such that the cooling influence of the Pacific is widely felt – and nowhere more so than in the 2001 AVA **Sta. Rita Hills** (the Chilean wine producer Santa Rita insists on the abbreviation), which is just a few miles inland from the coast and is really pretty chilly, thanks to sea fogs and wind, even in midsummer. As you move inland from here through the encompassing **Santa Ynez Valley** AVA, temperatures rise so that the easternmost AVA within it, **Happy Canyon**, specializes in full-blooded red bordeaux blends. There is constant competition between Santa Ynez Valley and **Santa Maria Valley** to the north of it. Santa Maria Valley is a little flatter and cooler, with some vast vineyards, including the Bien Nacido Vineyard, a 2,000-acre stretch of carefully tended green, surrounded by other fruit and vegetable crops. Between Santa Maria and Santa Ynez Valleys is many a vineyard around the little town of Los Alamos, much of which is shipped north to fill bottles carrying the names of many of California's bigger producers.

Oregon [R: Pinot Noir W: Pinot Gris, Chardonnay] Just as Sonoma is 'not Napa', Oregon is famously 'not California'. Pinot Noir has long dominated. The climate is much cooler, greyer and wetter, and the wine producers much smaller and right on, and less commercial. Sustainable production methods took hold here relatively early, despite the disease pressure of a damp climate. Oregon's heartland is the Willamette Valley (emphasis on the short A), where vineyards are surrounded by firs. For the minority white wines, Pinot Gris was the original variety of choice, but the quality of Oregon Chardonnay has been increasingly exciting as clones from Burgundy have been coming onstream.

Washington [R: Cabernet Sauvignon, Merlot, Syrah W: Chardonnay, Riesling] The hinterland of Seattle over the Cascades is basically a desert but, thanks to the Columbia and other rivers, it grows myriad crops, including apples and now grapes, so that Washington is the second wine-producing state of the US, albeit on a very much smaller scale than California. Winters are so cold here that vines may occasionally be fatally affected by low temperatures. The fruit in Washington wines is particularly bright throughout the wide array of varieties planted. Red bordeaux blends are a particular speciality, although from the mid 2000s, partly thanks to the determination of the dominant producer, Chateau Ste Michelle, there has been an effort to position Washington as a major producer of Riesling. Syrah can also be lip-smacking.

REST OF THE WORLD

PORTUGAL

[R: Aragonez/Tinta Roriz (Tempranillo), Castelão/João de Santarem/Perequita, Touriga Franca, Trincadeira/Tinta Amarela, Touriga Nacional, Baga, Tinta Barroca W: Síria/Roupeiro, Arinto/Pedernã, Loureir] Look at that list of Portugal's most planted grape varieties! The sheer number of local, unfamiliar names and synonyms indicates, accurately, how distinctive Portugal is as a wine producer. There is admittedly a little Cabernet and Chardonnay planted, but basically Portugal has remained true to its unique character. The wines tend to be drier and firmer than those made across the Spanish border, with the acid and tannin more in evidence. Many of the most exciting wines are in the north: Vinho Verde, mainly nervy whites sold on export markets, in the far north; the stunning wines of the equally stunning Douro valley (both sweet fortified purple port in all its guises and table wines of both colours from the same grape varieties); long-lived Dão, with Touriga Nacional a speciality; and Bairrada from the uncompromising Baga grape. All of these last three wines are usually red, but great white wine is increasingly easy to find. The Douro valley is one of the wine world's most haunting places – with virtually nothing but spectacular vineyards and the odd wine farm, or *quinta*, perched high above the river. Vintage port, made from a single, superior year, is the grandest sort, but needs decades of bottle age before it really shows its stuff. Arguably better value are single-quinta vintage ports, earlier-maturing wines made from one of the better wine farms. Ports matured for years in casks rather than bottles are called tawnies and tend to be paler and browner than the young, simpler purple ports known as rubies.

GERMANY

[R: Spätburgunder (Pinot Noir) W: Riesling, Müller-Thurgau] A revolution has taken place in German wine, but, alas, not enough wine drinkers outside Germany realize it. Sweet whites are now in a minority. Thanks to climate change, grapes now ripen fully and don't need added sweetness to distract from the tartness of unripe grapes. This is the home of the noble but uncompromising Riesling grape (see pp. 69–70), which grows in all regions but arguably reaches its miraculously delicate apogee in the Mosel valley, where some examples are less than 10 % alcohol yet can age for decades. Wines from regions with the word Rhein (Rhine) in their name, and from Pfalz, tend to be a bit heftier, having been grown further south. But Germany today is also making exciting substantial, often oaked, dry whites from Grauburgunder (Pinot Gris) and Weissburgunder (Pinot Blanc) as well as continuing the long tradition of making fine earthy Silvaner in the distinctly continental Franken region. Müller-Thurgau is a rather dreary, early-ripening grape variety that was much more popular when Riesling had difficulty ripening. It is, thank goodness, on the wane. Waxing rapidly, however, is a wide variety of red wine grapes (including even Cabernet Sauvignon and Syrah). The red burgundy grape is the most popular and can make increasingly fine wines, particularly across the Rhine from Alsace in Baden, although demand for them within Germany helps keep prices relatively high. The Germans keep tinkering with their quality designations. Basically look for the grape, the year, the producer and the region – but note that a wine with the word 'Auslese' on the label (especially as part of another word) will be sweet.

AUSTRIA

[R: Zweigelt, Blaufränkisch W: Grüner Veltliner, Welschriesling, Müller-Thurgau, Riesling] Austrians are, with good reason, hugely proud of the high average quality of their wines. Grüner Veltliner, grown throughout wine country in eastern Austria, is their own signature variety and makes full-bodied but very precise, appetising wines with strong aromas suggestive (to me) of dill pickle and white pepper. Welschriesling is unrelated to the Riesling of Germany and, although Germans look down their noses at it, can make some very good wine, some of it richly sweet, in Austria's Burgenland round the lake Neusiedlersee – particularly when blended with some Chardonnay. Müller-Thurgau is generally dreary here too, but some stunning, and geographically precise, Riesling is made, especially on the Danube in the Wachau, Kremstal and Kamptal wine regions. Nervy Sauvignon Blanc is a speciality of Steiermark (Styria) in the far south-east. Like many countries, Austria went through a love affair with oak and international grape varieties, but it now realizes how expressive its own, refreshing Blaufränkisch can be, if sensitively oaked. Zweigelt is a juicy, super-fruity, less serious speciality.

NORTHERN EUROPE

Thanks to climate change, the vine is spreading towards the poles where it can (the northern hemisphere). **England** now has an increasingly respectable wine industry, concentrated for obvious reasons in the south of the country. The **Benelux** countries are all serious wine producers nowadays, and even **Denmark** and **Sweden** produce some wine.

CENTRAL AND EASTERN EUROPE AND BEYOND

The wines of **Switzerland** have improved hugely in recent years but, alas, tend to be too expensive to export in any quantity. EU funds have been lavished on upgrading vine-yards and wineries in much of eastern Europe. Two of the most interesting wine-producing countries today are Slovenia (see Friuli, p. 85) and, especially, **Croatia,** which produces intriguing dry whites from its Malvazija grapes. Croatia has also turned out to be the original home of the grape that Californians know as Zinfandel and Puglians as Primitivo. **Serbia** is also starting to make some impressive international varietals. **Hungary** has its own very particular grapes and wine styles, most famously the long-lived sweet Tokai, now supplemented by dry varietal Furmint from the same grapes grown in the far north-east of the country. **Bulgaria** is producing some genuinely fine wine, mainly from international varieties, and **Romania,** with some rather more interesting grape varieties of its own, is catching up fast. Neighbouring **Moldova** has massive potential, and extensive plantings of international varieties, but is hampered by severe economic constraints. It will be a while before **Ukraine** exports much wine, particularly since it has lost its most promising wine region, the Crimea, to **Russia** – most of whose winters are too cold for wine production to be easy. A tiny amount of interesting red makes its way out of **Armenia,** but the really interesting wine producer is **Georgia,** where wine is completely embedded in the culture and religion. A host of indigenous vines yield fascinating flavours, enhanced by the tradition of fermenting grapes in buried earthenware vessels called *qvevri*.

EASTERN MEDITERRANEAN

Like Portugal, **Greece** has gone its own way and produces a host of very particular wine styles from indigenous grapes – many of them from the islands. Contrary to expectations from such a southerly European country, many of the finest wines are white, such as the Assyrtikos of Santorini and the local specialities of Crete. In the Middle Ages, sweet wines from Greece were some of the most highly valued of all. The birthplace of viticulture is thought to be somewhere between Anatolia in eastern **Turkey** and Georgia and, like Greece, Turkey has its own strong wine culture. It emerged briefly on the international scene a few years ago but is struggling somewhat under the current political regime. It is an irony that so much Middle Eastern land with some of the earliest links to viticulture is currently subject to strict Islamist rule. **Lebanon** is a delightful exception to all this, however, and fine wines, hearty reds and some intriguing rosés continue to emerge, somehow, from the vineyards of the Bekaa Valley, no matter how close to the war zones of Syria. To the south, **Israel** has spawned a lively wine culture, in the image of California's (with pricing to match, alas). The vineyards and cellars of **Cyprus** are being upgraded. I continue to hold my breath.

CANADA
[R: Pinot Noir, Cabernet Sauvignon W: Chardonnay, Vidal]
There are thousands of miles between the two major wine-producing provinces of Canada. Ontario's wine country is centred on Niagara, just north of the famous Falls. It made its name making Icewine, sweet wine made from frozen grapes, because winters are so cold–though slightly less cold than they used to be. And summers are now hot enough to ripen grapes fully–even some Cabernets. Ontario Chardonnay and sparkling wine can be really very convincing.

British Columbia also makes a substantial amount of wine, mainly on the much-photographed shores of the lake in Okanagan Valley. Most international varieties are grown here, and flavours are particularly fruity and sharp–not totally dissimilar to the wines made across the border in Washington state.

SOUTH AMERICA

Argentina [R: Malbec, Bonarda, Cabernet Sauvignon W: Chardonnay, Torrontés] As well as the grape varieties listed here, Argentina grows vast quantities of pink-skinned grapes that go into very basic wines for domestic consumption. But rich, ripe, velvety, spicy Malbec is Argentina's signature wine, a wine that is much more popular (especially in North America) than the Malbec grown in its birthplace, Cahors in south-west France. Most of Argentina's vineyards are in the foothills of the Andes, whose melted snows have long provided the irrigation needed for viticulture. Elevation and the moderation of temperature that goes with it counterbalance the low latitudes here, and it is not uncommon for producers to cite on wine labels specific vineyard elevations (usually above 1,000 metres, when 500 metres is widely regarded as the viable maximum in Europe). Although red wines are much more common, Argentina also produces some pretty smart Chardonnay–a bit like a somehow 'stonier' version of California examples. Heady, perfumed, rather full-bodied whites from Torrontés grapes are another speciality.

Chile [R: Cabernet Sauvignon, Merlot W: Chardonnay, Sauvignon Blanc] Chile's wine industry is currently in flux. It was originally based around the capital, Santiago, just over the Andes from Argentina's principal wine city Mendoza, but is now rapidly spreading the considerable length of this long, thin country. Perhaps because of its relative isolation, Chile is relatively free of vine pests and diseases, and the climate with its reliable sunshine and (until recently) the plentiful supply of irrigation has seemed ideal for vine growing. When quantity was more important than quality, vineyards were concentrated in the fertile Central Valley, but nowadays Chile's ambitious wine producers have been establishing new wine regions closer to the cooling influence of the Pacific, in the far south and north, and ever higher up into the mountains. Until very recently Chile produced only international varieties, and production was strictly controlled by a handful of Chile's most powerful families, but a new generation of wine producers has emerged who are taking advantage of old, unirrigated vines in such southerly regions as Maule and Itata.

Brazil and **Uruguay** also make respectable wines, with Uruguay specializing in the Tannat grape imported by Basque immigrants.

SOUTH AFRICA

[R: Cabernet Sauvignon, Shiraz/Syrah, Pinotage W: Chenin Blanc, Colombard, Sauvignon Blanc, Chardonnay] As in Chile, the South African wine scene has been revitalized by a new wave of producers making wines that are definitively South African rather than local copies of French classics. Old bush-vines planted between the wheatfields of arid, inland Swartland are the most common raw material, in stark contrast to the much more manicured vineyards of Stellenbosch, Franschhoek and Paarl, which are more likely to be planted with irrigated international varieties. But, again as in Chile, there has also been a flight to the cooling influence of the coast, and in some cases higher elevations. Another attribute shared with Chile is great value in the wide range of wine styles and flavours available, from a country that has definitively emerged from its political isolation but is still finding its way towards a genuinely equal society.

AUSTRALIA

[R: Shiraz, Cabernet Sauvignon W: Chardonnay] Wine is hugely important to Australian culture, and it is produced in most Australian regions that are cool and wet enough to grow good quality grapes, as well as in some hot inland regions that depend on irrigation. From a standing start in the late 1980s, Australia has become one of the world's most active wine exporters and a major player in wine research and development. But it has almost become a victim of its own success, because so many wine drinkers associate the country with wine technology and the mass market. In fact, there are pockets of fine-wine production throughout southern Australia, a result of great natural conditions and both skill and determination in cellar and vineyard. Sunny (though increasingly slimline of late) Chardonnay and bargain Shiraz from corporate behemoths tell only a small part of the tale. Hunter Valley Semillon, super-sweet oak-aged fortified wines, the steely Rieslings of Clare and Eden valleys, sun-baked Barossa Shiraz, fine Pinots from Mornington Peninsula, Yarra Valley and Tasmania, Margaret River Cabernets and Sauvignon/Semillon blends, and confident offerings from all over South Australia and Victoria are the more interesting and definitively Australian ingredients in the story. The best have tended to be made by the many dedicated and proficient family-run wine companies throughout Australia, and they are now being supplemented, sometimes challenged, by a new generation of producers, influenced by the natural-wine movement and geographical specificity above all else. These are exciting times for those prepared to look beyond the supermarket bargain bin. And after losing patience with poor-quality corks, Australia, like New Zealand, aims most of its wines at those who love the convenience of screwcaps.

NEW ZEALAND

[R: Pinot Noir W: Sauvignon Blanc] No nation is prouder of their country's wines than the Kiwis, and NZ Sauvignon Blanc is a popular favourite not just with them but with Aussies and Brits too. It's rather tempting to say that the two grapes listed above tell most of the story of NZ wine, so dedicated are vine growers – and many consumers – to these two varieties. The North and particularly South Islands have had huge commercial success with their user-friendly style of Sauvignon Blanc (see pp. 68 – 9), the speciality of the vastly expanded Marlborough region. Crisp acidity and exuberant fruit flavours are the hallmarks of Kiwi wine that are particularly easy to appreciate. An increasing number of producers are now managing to make wines with a bit of subtlety and longevity too.

ASIA

Vines are sprouting all over Asia, sometimes in the most unlikely places, thanks to the popularity of wine as a drink, leisure interest and status symbol. The most dramatic growth has been in **China**, which, according to its own statistics, is now rivalling the US as home to the world's fourth biggest vineyard area.

New World v. Old World

Towards the end of the twentieth century we winos were rather obsessed by the differences between European wine producers and the rest, noting that Old World wines were likely to be initially more reticent, and then longer living, than their New World counterparts. Old World wines were all labelled with geographical place names, so-called appellations, while New World wines were labelled varietally, by grape. New World wines were more likely to be the product of technology, whereas horny-handed men of the soil still ruled the roost in European wine regions. Waves of flying winemakers swept through the less-celebrated cellars of Europe preaching the gospel that, among desirable wine attributes, cleanliness was next to fruitiness.

But in the twenty-first century the differences between Europeans and the rest have become much less marked. Virtually every aspiring wine producer, wherever they are, travels to gain experience somewhere completely different and, thanks to the internet, ends up with a network of contacts all over the wine world. Everyone learns something from others. Everyone, wherever they are, seems to have the same sort of ideals: to transmit the expression of place as accurately as possible with minimal intervention in the winery. Wine quality is no longer measured by the number of new small oak barrels its producer buys each year, nor by how ripe the grapes were when they were picked. Alcohol levels are coming down. Big old oak and concrete are more fashionable than new oak. And that is true for most wine producers wherever they are.

Wine jargon

An insider's guide to vino-lingo.

acid, acidity an essential ingredient in any drink that keeps it refreshing and wards off harmful bacteria. See 'How to taste' and 'Common tasting terms' (pp. 25–33)

additives most wine has a little sulphur added to it; industrial wines may have a wide range of chemical additives including yeast nutrients, acids, tannins and preservatives. Roll on ingredient listing for wines, I say

alcohol without it, wine would be fruit juice. Fermentation turns the sugars in grapes into alcohol

appellation a controlled geographical designation: at least, a legally specified area, as in American Viticultural Areas, which may extend over millions of acres; at most (as in France's appellations known as AOCs or AOPs) a set of regulations that dictate not just where the wine comes from but exactly how the vines are grown, which varieties in which proportions, how the grapes are harvested and how the wines are made and aged. Italian appellations are called DOC and DOCG, Spanish ones DO.

assemblage usually used to denote the precise proportions of different grape varieties in a wine; also used for the process of blending the new vintage of a wine, particularly in smart bordeaux

blind tasting tasting wine without knowing what it is you are tasting. Tasting semi-blind can be tasting a range of wines when you know what is in the selection but not which wine is which

bottle age the quality of having evolved as a result of time spent maturing in bottle. This has no direct relation to **vintage**; it is simply what happens to the wine as a result of spending time in the bottle. The constituents have had time to interact and create more interesting compounds and the tannins are precipitated out so that the wine tastes less tough

breathing some people believe that opening a bottle and letting the wine stand allows the wine to 'breathe' before serving. See 'When to open the bottle – and whether to decant' (pp. 60–1)

carbon dioxide the gas given off during **fermentation**; found dissolved in sparkling wines

carbonic maceration winemaking technique designed to produce particularly fruity, low-tannin wines by fermenting whole grapes in a sealed tank; once much used in Beaujolais, and in the Languedoc-Roussillon for softening wines made from tough Carignan grapes

chaptalization adding sugar to the **must** before **fermentation** to increase the final level of **alcohol** in the wine. See 'How strong is my wine?' (pp. 22–3)

château wine estates in Bordeaux tend to be called châteaux (French for castles), however modest

claret traditional British term for red bordeaux; it generally denotes a relatively light-bodied wine with a decent amount of tannin and acidity in youth

classed growth for the Paris Exhibition of 1855, the Bordeaux wine brokers classified what were then the top sixty châteaux, or **crus**, into five divisions on the basis of their selling prices; believe it or not, this system still operates today, as in 'first growth' (the best) down to 'fifth growth'

clone a family of vines all derived, by clonal selection, for particular attributes such as **yield**, disease resistance or colour, from a single mother vine. Compare **massal selection**

commune French name for a parish. In Italian it's *comune*.

cru literally means 'growth', so a Premier Cru is a first growth – pretty special in Burgundy, with Grand Cru being even more so. In Italy a cru is a special vineyard with demonstrable character while a Cru Beaujolais comes from one of the ten superior communes (see p. 80)

cru classé French for **classed growth**

cuve close literally, 'sealed tank' – the French name for the tank method of making wine sparkling

domaine the Burgundy equivalent of Bordeaux's **château**, a (usually quite small) wine estate, typically in Burgundy consisting of a few rows of vines in several different vineyards, each of a different **appellation**

fermentation the process of transforming grape sugars into **alcohol** and **carbon dioxide** under the influence of **yeast**

field blend a mix of different grape varieties planted in the same vineyard; some wines may be made from a field blend

horizontal tasting tasting of (usually related) wines from a single vintage

massal selection a mix of plants of the same variety but with different qualities

mis(e) en bouteille au domaine/château French for 'bottled at the estate [that grew the grapes]' – A Good Thing

must the soup that is halfway between grape juice and wine; it may contain skins, pips and fragments of the grape stems

natural wine fashionable wine containing minimal additives (see p. 55)

non-vintage a wine that is not the produce of a single year, so a blend of more than one **vintage** (such blends account for well over 90 % of all the champagne sold), or, in cheap wines, a wine that does not carry a vintage so that the same label can be used no matter what the blend and age of the wine

orange wine white wine fermented (like a red wine) in
contact with the grape skins so that it has a particularly
deep colour, and is relatively astringent
petit château one of the hundreds of smaller, less glamorous châteaux in Bordeaux
sparkling wine what fizzy wines other than champagne
are called
still wine wine that is not **sparkling wine**
TCA short for trichloroanisole, the most common cause
of the mould that causes cork taint (see p. 38)
traditional method the classic way of making champagne,
much imitated elsewhere
varietal the adjective from **variety**; used chiefly to describe
wines made from a single stated grape variety
variety grape varieties within a single vine species, usually
Vitis vinifera
vertical tasting tasting of different vintages of the same
wine
vintage wine term for the single year in which a wine was
harvested, as opposed to a **non-vintage** wine, which may
be made from a blend of wines made in more than one
year. Thus in the northern hemisphere wine is the product of the growing season of that year, because the grape
harvest (also called the vintage) typically takes place in
September or October, whereas the growing season in
the southern hemisphere, where grapes are picked
around February and March, extends over the previous
calendar year as well.
Vitis vinifera the European vine species responsible for
almost all the wine made today. A species comes in mul-
tiple different varieties – as for all plants. American vine
species tend to make wines with a very distinctive taste.
The Concord grape, responsible for most American

grape juice and jelly, is the most widely planted American variety

yeast tiny and very varied fungi that have the power to transform grape sugars into **alcohol**. Yeast present in the atmosphere of a winery or vineyard can be responsible for what's called a spontaneous or wild fermentation, which some think results in more characterful wines; but the results are not predictable, whereas cultured yeasts, specially selected for various attributes, are associated with fewer risks

yield the amount of wine or grapes produced per unit of vineyard area. In Europe this is typically expressed as hectolitres (1 hectolitre = 100 litres) per hectare, whereas outside Europe tonnes of grapes per acre are a more common measurement of yield. In general, the lower the yield, the more concentrated the wine, but vines are generally happier and better balanced if very low yields are not imposed on them, typically by savage pruning.

Where to Find Out More

To keep expanding your wine education, see:

JancisRobinson.com Updated daily, with well over 125,000 tasting notes and over 10,000 articles, about a third of which are free

The World Atlas of Wine, **7th edition** The world of wine mapped in detail, with hand-picked labels and explanatory text

The Oxford Companion to Wine, **4th edition** Almost a million words made up of alphabetically listed articles on 4,000 wine-related topics, including history, geography, grape varieties, science, and leading people and producers

Wine Grapes: A Complete Guide to 1,386 Vine Varieties Including Their Origins and Flavours Everything you need to know about the grapes that produce wines

Mastering Wine – Jancis Robinson's Shortcuts to Success A video wine course on Udemy.com

See also
www.24hourwineexpert.com
for more detail related to this book including specific wine recommendations.